HOPEFUL IMAGINATION

*Also by Walter Brueggemann and
published by SCM Press*

The Prophetic Imagination

Walter Brueggemann
HOPEFUL IMAGINATION

PROPHETIC VOICES IN EXILE

SCM PRESS LTD

224

Biblical quotations, unless otherwise noted, are from the Revised
Standard Version of the Bible, copyright 1946, 1952, © 1971, 1973
by the Division of Christian Education of the National Council of
the Churches of Christ in the U.S.A. and are used by permission.

ISBN 0 334 02528 1

First published in Great Britain 1992
by SCM Press Ltd
26–30 Tottenham Road, London N1 4BZ

Typeset in the United States of America
and printed in Great Britain by
Mackays of Chatham PLC, Chatham, Kent

To Eden Faculty Colleagues
Past and Present
with whom I have shared
and from whom I have received life

CONTENTS

PREFACE

THIS BOOK SEEKS to do two interpretive tasks at the same time. First, it attempts to do biblical theology, to discern and articulate the main theological claims of a body of textual material, to listen to the text, and to speak echoes of it. Second, the book seeks to make a hermeneutical move to our own theological situation by drawing a "dynamic equivalent" between Israel's exilic situation and that of the American church. Thus an effort is made to address both "what it meant" and "what it means." In working at both tasks, it has seemed clear that while the two are distinct tasks, they cannot be completely separated. I have come to think it is inevitable that one's sense of "what it means" will impinge on "what it meant." I suspect that biblical theology that has any vitality is always done in this way.

These chapters are a combination of two series of lectures. Portions of the manuscript were first presented at a Pastors' Conference to the pastors of the Missouri Conference, United Church of Christ, at which I was hosted by my bishops, Rueben Koehler and David Felton. These lectures eventually were formalized as the Scott Lectures at Brite Divinity School, Texas Christian University, where I was graciously hosted by Dean M. Jack Suggs. Other parts of the manuscript were presented to the Pastors' Conference of the Board of Homeland Ministries, United Church of Christ, where I was hosted by Robert Burtt and George Worcester, and were finally presented as the Schaff lectures at Pittsburgh Theological Seminary. There I was warmly hosted by President Samuel Calien, Dean Ulrich Mauser, and especially by my friend Professor Jared J. Jackson. I express my gratitude to all of these people who have affirmed my efforts and believed in my work. It is important for me, and no doubt telling for their casting, that the lectures in both series began by the process of thinking with the pastors of the church and ended with more formal academic presentations. I suspect that is how my mind works about Scripture interpretation. I submit that is a fair way to work, given the double responsibility for church and for academy.

My ability to bring the lectures to this book form owes a special debt to three persons. Donna LaGrasso has been patient and thoughtful about typing and retyping. My colleague Gail O'Day has scrutinized the text in its argument and in its articulation and has decidedly strengthened the argument and improved its presentation. John A. Hollar of Fortress Press continues to be for me a powerful support, because he cares not only about the selling of books in quantity, but the writing of books in quality. To all three, I express my gratitude.

This book has been for me both a scholarly enterprise as well as a sustained probe concerning the shape of faithfulness in the church tradition of the United Church of Christ. In that latter enterprise, Mary Miller Brueggemann has been an engaged conversation partner and I am grateful.

The completion of this book comes at the close of a season in my life. This is the final book-length manuscript I will complete as a member of the faculty of Eden Theological Seminary. After twenty-five years in such a faculty, departure is not without pain, sadness, and wistfulness. In thanksgiving and celebration I offer this book as a gift to my Eden faculty colleagues, past and present, with whom I have shared so much of my life. They have been patient and caring, confrontive and supportive. Some of them have been peculiarly decisive in shaping my life, my faith, my vocation, my scholarship, my angle of vision, and my methods of work. They know who they are and what they have done for me. I am deeply grateful. That precious memory of colleagueship will continue to be a main force of possibility for me.

WALTER BRUEGGEMANN

Eden Theological Seminary
September 30, 1985

INTRODUCTION: EXILE AND THE VOICE OF HOPE

NEW POETIC IMAGINATION

THE TRADITIONS OF Jeremiah, Ezekiel, and 2 Isaiah constitute a remarkable literary achievement. They invite us to a stunning theological exploration, for they embody some of the boldest and most eloquent theological probing in the Old Testament.[1]

This literature is from a period when the "known world" of Jerusalem was assaulted and finally disbanded. In 587 Jerusalem was destroyed, and with it the symbols and props which held life together.[2] That ending could be understood politically as a result of Babylonian expansionism or theologically as the end of Yahweh's patience with this people. While the biblical literature is certainly not unaware of the former political explanation, it focuses deliberately and almost exclusively on the latter theological point. Thus, Babylonian expansionism is subordinated to and explained in terms of Yahweh's judgment (Jer. 25:9, 27:6). These three poetic traditions of Jeremiah, Ezekiel, and 2 Isaiah are cast in the difficult role of providing voice and articulation to the faith and experience of this community in a very odd circumstance. The governing metaphor for this literature is that of *exile*. In this brief definitive period in Old Testament faith, pastoral responsibility was to help people *enter into exile*, to be *in exile*, and *depart out of exile*.

Gerhard von Rad has seen that the poetry in the tradition of Jeremiah, Ezekiel, and 2 Isaiah embodies a most peculiar and important disjunction in the traditions of the Old Testament. Indeed, this

1

insight is crucial to the way in which von Rad has structured the two volumes of his *Old Testament Theology*, with the hinge coming out of Isa. 43:18–19:

> Do not remember former things.
> Behold, I am doing a new thing.[3]

Up until this point in the faith and history of Israel, the poets and prophets had continually turned back to the old traditions and articulated their enduring relevance.[4] Von Rad has seen that these three poets, more than any others, do not base their appeal on the continuing power of the old tradition but in fact enunciate new actions of God that are discontinuous with the old traditions.[5] They proclaim a new beginning with fresh actions from God that are wrought in this moment of exile, in this crisis of dismantling. Two comments need to be made about that discernment. First, these new actions of God which they articulate are not new actions that were obvious on the face of it. That is why the poet asks with astonished impatience, "Do you not perceive it?" (Isa. 43:19) They were actions that were discernable and spoken precisely by these persons with their enormous *prophetic imagination*. These poets not only *discerned* the new actions of God that others did not discern, but they *wrought* the new actions of God by the power of their imagination, their tongues, their words. New poetic imagination evoked new realities in the community.

Second, as von Rad and Walther Zimmerli have shown so well, the matter of the end of the old tradition and the presentation of new actions is a dialectical matter. The actions of God are new, but they are cast largely in the molds and images of the old memories so that the discernment and presentation of the new depend profoundly on knowledge about the old. These speakers present for Israel a new reading of historical reality that is really "there" in the public process, but it is not fully present until brought to imaginative speech.

The imaginative speech of this literature that makes the present freshly available is speech that grows out of the memory of Israel. This new literature is not personal invention. Rather, these poets probe and mine the tradition in ways that cause the old tradition to articulate a newness. It is probable that both the form and substance of the new articulation are shaped by the liturgical practices of Israel, for it is in the liturgy that Israel kept its past present. These poets live in tension with liturgical practice, both utilizing and criticizing its claims.

This literature is so powerful, so unsettling, and so buoyant because these poets have tongues and imagination adequate to bring to speech what is happening to Judah. They have the capacity and boldness to speak about the loss in ways that require their listeners to face the nullification wrought by God. But they also have the remarkable ability to speak a new world beyond the loss of 587. No doubt there were exhausted, despairing people around these three poets who saw nothing new, who hoped nothing new, and who could speak nothing new. The newness which von Rad so celebrates depends on the ability of these poets to speak a newness out beyond the limits of the purview of their contemporaries.[6]

Thus we study the themes, metaphors, and dynamics which give new life to the tradition, which summon to faith in a fresh way, and which create hope for a community so deeply in crisis that it might have abandoned the entire enterprise of faith. This literature of realism and candor referred the loss to God and thereby released energy, courage, and passion in the community.

THE PIVOT—587 B.C.E.

The literature of Jeremiah, Ezekiel, and 2 Isaiah is a collection of many different kinds of rhetorical efforts, of varying shapes, no doubt offered in a variety of contexts. But that disordered mass of material has been subjected to a long editorial process which eventuated in the canonical shape of the material as we have it. That editorial process has served to order and thematize the material. While the intentionality of the order is not always clear to us, we can identify the thematization which is behind the editorial process.[7] The literature as it has now been shaped is intended to help the community of faith make two crucial and difficult moves, *relinquishment* and *receiving*.

In understanding this literature, the date and events of 587 B.C.E. are decisive. The year 587 is the occasion when the temple in Jerusalem was burned, the holy city was destroyed, the Davidic dynasty was terminated, the leading citizens deported. Public life in Judah came to an end. Our interest, however, is not in the descriptive character of a historical event. Rather our study is organized around "587" now treated as metaphor. We will refer to that date as a way of speaking about the end of any known world, about the dismantling of any system of meaning and power. By breaking the reference loose from its "facticity," the literature around 587 becomes available for other analogous situations.[8] The experience of ending and dismantlement may be charted in this way:

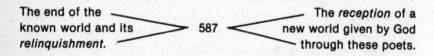

The end of the known world and its *relinquishment*. → 587 ← The *reception* of a new world given by God through these poets.

Judah had two tasks in this crisis of life and faith. It had to let go of the old world of king and temple that God had now taken from it. It had to receive from God's hand a new world which it did not believe possible and which was not the one it would have preferred or chosen.

These three poets of enormous freedom, courage, and imagination take as their proper work aiding the community in relinquishing and receiving.[9] They speak of God's intrusive and abrasive governance, which takes away what is treasured but has become unacceptable to God. And they speak inventively of the new gifts of God, which surprisingly make a new form of life possible in the world, just when all seemed ended and beyond recall.

RELINQUISHMENT AND RECEIVING

The world is perceived under the twin aspects of *relinquishment* and *receiving*.[10] That perception of reality is based in an unshakeable theological conviction: God's powerful governance is displacing the present idolatrous order of public life and is generating a new order that befits God's will for the world. This theological conviction is not rooted in political observation, economic analysis, or cultural yearning. It is rooted decisively in the notion of who God is and what God wills.

The world that God wills is held to be in profound tension and finally in opposition to the present ordering of reality in seventh-century Jerusalem. Thus the sovereignty of God will lead to the harsh end of present sociopolitical arrangements. The latter are based on a reason that controls, on an economics that monopolizes, on a politics that pretends autonomy. These are embodied in the political claims of the Davidic dynasty, in the ritual pretensions of the Jerusalem priesthood and temple, and in the public arrangements of power, practiced and trusted in the royal temple system of Jerusalem.

The sovereignty of God, however, is presented not simply as a norm for criticism. These poets speak not only of relinquishment. Yahweh's sovereignty is a powerful source of hope. It is announced that God's faithful people may expect to receive from God a new mode of public existence. Life can begin again in a new community that is trustfully obedient to the norms of covenant.

Such a theological reading of reality, one which envisions the destruction of idols and the emergence of new community, will inevitably evoke resistance. These poetic traditions do indeed subvert conventional readings of reality and conventional arrangements of power. These traditions evidence the process in ancient Israel of presenting and making available an alternative world that often seemed unwelcome and unreal. Its welcome and its reality are based only on the conviction that God's resolution of Israel's history is one to embrace in obedience and to celebrate in praise. Such obedience and praise are a practice of a dangerous alternative and a rejection of a world designed apart from and against the rule of God.

This study is preoccupied with the three biblical traditions of Jeremiah, Ezekiel, and 2 Isaiah. But it is also undertaken in the conviction that these biblical traditions touch very closely to our own situation of faith. The analogy to "587" which keeps emerging in this study is that we also, at the end of the twentieth century, are engaged in a process through which God is ending our "known world" and inviting us to a new world of obedience and praise.

A variety of scholars are calling attention to the prospect that Enlightenment modes of power and Enlightenment modes of knowledge are at the end of their effective rule among us.[11] All of us are children of the Enlightenment. That cultural reality of the last 250 years has brought us enormous gifts of human reason, human freedom, and human possibility. None of us would want to undo those gifts, but they are gifts not without cost. The reality of the

Enlightenment has also resulted in the concentration of power in monopolistic ways which have been uncriticized. Moreover, it has generated dominating models of knowledge which have been thought to be objective rather than dominating.

The evidence grows that the long-standing concentration of power and knowledge which constitutes our human world is under heavy assault and in great jeopardy. God's work at transforming our world is apparent in the rise of Third World nations, the emergence of Islam as a vigorous political force, and the visibility of a variety of liberation movements. In the midst of such realities, we discover the ineffectiveness of old modes of power. American military and economic power is of course considerable, but it is not everywhere decisive. The limit of such power is matched by the limit of Enlightenment modes of knowledge, for we are coming to see that such "scientific" knowledge no longer carries authority everywhere. There is increasing suspicion of such knowledge because it has long been in the service of domination. Such knowledge arranges reality in ways that are not disinterested. Technique becomes a mode of control, and that mode is no longer easily or universally embraced.

Trust in these conventional modes of power and knowledge is matched by a growing uneasiness when those modes are critiqued or rejected. My argument is that the loss of the authority of the dynasty and temple in Jerusalem is analogous to the loss of certainty, dominance, and legitimacy in our own time. In both cases the relinquishment is heavy and costly.[12]

The reception of a new world from God is also under way in our time. It takes such concrete form as land reform whereby peasants receive again their birthright. It is apparent in the staggering, frightening emergence of new communities, which we experience as revolutionary, with dreams of justice and equity. Those dangerous emergences are paralleled by dreams of justice and mercy in our culture that dare to affirm that old structures may be transformed to be vehicles for the new gifts of God. Thus we are at the risky point of receiving from God what we thought God would not give, namely a new way to be human in the world.

Focus on these three prophetic traditions is thus intended to help us think through our own situation and our own vocation as a community of obedience and praise. Our situation also is one of loss and gift. Our vocation is *to relinquish and receive*, and to help others to do so. But that vocation is not simply one of "social action," which might be suggested by such grand themes as relinquishment and reception. Ours is equally a vocation of pastoral action and pastoral care.[13] For the great moves that God is working in the public arena impinge upon every aspect of personal life as well. Relinquishment and reception cut through every dimension of life, for such moves entail nothing less than dying in order to be raised to new life.

In the end, this book intends to be a contribution to a discussion about vitality in ministry. My sense is that the ministry of the American church is in many ways fatigued and close to despair. That is so because we are double-minded. On the one hand, we have some glimpses of the truth of God's gospel of relinquishment and reception, and we see where it may lead us in terms of social reality. On the other hand, the church is so fully enmeshed in the dominant values of our culture that freedom for action is difficult. In any case, it is evident that ministry will be freed of fatigue, despair, and cynicism only as we are able to see clearly what we are up to, and then perhaps able to act intentionally. Such intentionality is dangerous and problematic, but when and where the church acts with such freedom and courage, it finds the gift of new life is surprisingly given. It is toward that freedom and energy that this book is intended.

The book takes up in turn each of the three prophetic traditions of Jeremiah, Ezekiel, and 2 Isaiah. Two chapters are provided for each. The first in each pair is an attempt to articulate the interpretive problematic of the tradition in a general way. The second in each pair is an attempt to speak concretely with reference to a particular text. Attention to the text is an important responsibility for a ministry of relinquishment and reception, for it is the text that mediates the reality of loss and the power of newness. These texts live and speak very close to the reality of God's own grief and hope which may, when we are faithful, be embraced as our own grief and hope.

PART **1**

ONLY GRIEF
PERMITS NEWNESS

1

JEREMIAH—DESIGNED
FOR CONFLICT

JEREMIAH, EZEKIEL, AND 2 ISAIAH constitute three major
voices of exile and homecoming in Israel. We begin our study with
Jeremiah. The book of Jeremiah is a complex literary collection. It offers poignant poetry and plodding prose. It speaks harsh judgment
and inescapable destruction, but it also articulates passionate hope.

The tradition of Jeremiah is focused on the destiny of Jerusalem,
the beloved city which is to be destroyed—and then to be built again.
The literature of Jeremiah asserts this two-stage destiny for the city.
But it not only asserts. It also uses powerful language to "speak" the
city to its end and to its new, stunning beginning.

The Jeremiah literature is difficult to date with any precision, but it
can surely be located in the period just before and just after the
destruction of Jerusalem in 587 B.C.E. The great geopolitical fact of
this period is the rise and expansion of the Babylonian empire, which
posed a heavy and sustained threat against Jerusalem. It is the key insight of the Jeremiah tradition to see that the Babylonian threat embodies the judgment Yahweh has decreed against the city. That insight
is at the core of the Jeremiah tradition and it is that insight which put
Jeremiah profoundly at odds with his contemporaries. The conventional dates for the person of Jeremiah are 626–581. As for the date of
the literature of the book, some of it surely originates in the next
generation or two, among exiles.

In conventional scholarship it has been claimed and assumed that we know more about the prophet Jeremiah than any other prophet in the Old Testament. The most recent scholarship,[1] especially under the impetus of Ernest Nicholson and Robert Carroll,[2] has powerfully challenged that presupposition, so that now some scholars assert that we know as little about Jeremiah as any of the other prophets.[3] Such a lack of knowledge may be correct as a purely historical comment, but I am nonetheless troubled by such a conclusion and not fully convinced. It seems to be the case that Carroll is still asking traditional questions about "the historical Jeremiah," only he draws negative conclusions. A much more conservative position can be made concerning dating, as for example by John Bright[4] and William Holladay.[5] These scholars are much more inclined to ask about the date of the material in relation to the life and person of Jeremiah, and they do not focus on the exile as the generative period of the literature. These two views, a more traditional one which focuses on conventional historical questions and a more recent view which focuses on the late editing of the book, are at something of an impasse. The momentum of scholarship is in the direction of the more radical view of Nicholson and Carroll, with its propensity to move the literature into a later period. While that may be correct, there is something inherently problematic in a dating that speaks against a pervasive claim of the literature itself.

Perhaps the canonical view of Childs is a way out of the impasse.[6] Childs has urged that the Book of Jeremiah is shaped so that the early tradition of the prophet is presented as judgment, and the Deuteronomistic work in the book carries the theme of deliverance and rebuilding. The Book of Jeremiah as it now stands thus makes a statement about the juxtaposition of judgment and deliverance.[7]

In effect, Childs has bracketed out the historical questions. I am content to follow that suggestion in order to get on with the interpretive task at hand. Thus we will study, not the historical person of Jeremiah, but the voice of Jeremiah as it is heard and mediated through the text of the book, albeit a Deuteronomic mediation and portrayal. Of that portrayal we can know a great deal,[8] and with the presupposition of that portrayal we shall begin.

PASTORAL VITALITY AND
PASTORAL CONFLICT

Jeremiah as presented to us is a study in pastoral vitality and pastoral conflict. His work is precisely linked to the issues surrounding the crisis of 587. His task is to help his community to face the loss of the old world of king and temple and to receive a new world defined by Yahweh. That new world—experienced as exile—is shaped by Babylonian domination, which is willed by Yahweh. Jeremiah's contemporaries wanted neither to *lose* the old Davidic-Jerusalem world nor to *receive* a new world at the hands of the Babylonian empire. So they engaged in denial, self-deception, and wishful thinking.

The tradition traces with candor the conflicts in this prophetic life, which are not unlike our own. The tradition of Jeremiah knows from the beginning that Jeremiah is designed for conflict. This "over-against" quality of Jeremiah's ministry is anticipated in the call of Jer. 1:4–10, and it is explicit in vv. 15–19, which may indeed belong to the call tradition.[9] In vv. 15–16, Yahweh is first of all announced as one who is against the present world of Judah:

> I am calling all the tribes of the kingdoms of the north . . . *against* all its
> walls round about, *against* all the cities of Judah.
> And I will utter my judgment *against* them. (1:15–16)

Then Jeremiah is included in the againstness of God:

> But you . . . *against* the whole land, *against* the kings of Judah, *against*
> its princes, *against* its priests, *against* the people of the land.
> They will fight *against* you, but they will not prevail against you. (vv.
> 17–19; au. trans.)

The reason they will not prevail is "because I am with you to snatch you" (v. 19; au. trans.).[10] God is now dismantling the defended, presumed world of Jerusalem, the holy dynasty, the holy city, the holy temple.[11] From the outset it is clear that there will be resistance to the God who dismantles and to the prophet who carries the dismantling word. The resistance may be against the resolve of God, but experientially the resistance will be focused on Jeremiah who brings the message of God's resolve. Thus in his very call, Jeremiah is designed by God for conflict. That is his vocation and the sure shape of his call.

This way of speaking treats the call narrative as a report on a personal experience of the prophet. Norman Habel has shown how the passage is highly stylized and follows a standard form of call narrative.[12] I am aware of alternative interpretations: (1) that the narrative is a liturgical form (Reventlow),[13] and (2) that the unit functions to legitimate the task of the person.[14] Whichever of these interpretations is taken, the call narrative is useful to see the presupposition of conflict. The call narrative does not need to be understood in psychological, personalistic terms to see that it is a program for conflict. The conflict has theological roots that pervade the entire life of the prophet and the entire literature. It should not be trivialized as a momentary psychological experience. The call is precisely against the royal ideology of the day. Yahweh and Yahweh's prophet stand profoundly against the deceptively constructed world of king and temple.

The tradition knows Jeremiah is destined for conflict, because he is to be a party to the conflict between Yahweh and recalcitrant Jerusalem. Jeremiah's life, ministry, and literature are all shaped by this conflict. To counter that conflict, Jeremiah has only a promise, "I will be with you" (1:8, 19; cf. 15:20–21). It is a promise from God. But it is such a frail response in the face of such formidable adversaries. The religious question running beneath the polemic is whether the promise is adequate in the face of the conflict.

The reflective poetry of Jeremiah is aimed precisely at this interface of conflict and promised solidarity. The poet reflects on the strife and conflict that comes even in the face of innocence:

Woe is me, my mother, that you bore me, a man of strife and contention to the whole land! I have not lent, nor have I borrowed, yet all of them curse me. (15:10)

Then the poet asks a rhetorical question:

Can one break iron, iron from the north, and bronze? (v. 12)

The poet does not know if iron will prevail in such strife. The reference to iron would seem to be the irresistable power of the invading army from the north. Yet notice that in 1:18 it is precisely Jeremiah who is characterized as this unbreakable metal.[15]

Jeremiah thus seems to be asking, "Why am I always embroiled even though I am to blame for nothing?'' The answer given by the witness of the text is that Jeremiah is set for such conflict because he is summoned by God to tell the truth about the fundamentally false organization of life in Jerusalem. The truth is that the false reality is now to be ended and dismantled by the purpose of God. The main lines of his ministry are thus articulated. The wonder is that in the midst of the embroilment he is a man of uncommon vitality. This is not to say that he did not have doubt, depression, and failure of nerve. But in the main flow of his ministry, he did not succumb to denial, cynicism, or assimilation. We may identify the following reasons for his continuing vitality and passion, reasons which may be replicated and appropriated in our own situation.

Jeremiah has a robust view of God. Vitality for such a tough ministry as Jeremiah's is rooted in the God to whom the ministry belongs. The God of Jeremiah is no scholastic God who is bound by creeds and conventions. This is not a liberal God who is simply an echo of the community writ large. Nor is this God the patron of the royal temple establishment. This God is a vital, free conversation partner to whom Jeremiah can speak candidly and who surely is free to say anything back to Jeremiah.

This vitality in Jeremiah's knowledge of God is evident in his prayer life which is essentially *combative*.[16] In these verses we are given some of the most eloquent and abrasive prayers of the Bible. The confessions of Jeremiah constitute a special corpus of powerful poems.[17] Jeremiah's prayer speech is anything but serene solidarity. Jeremiah takes the other side against God and even in prayer assumes an adversarial posture.[18] Jeremiah may be a voice of disappointment, forlornness, and hostility, but in that very voice, the vitality of God is present and known.

The robustness of God is evident in Jeremiah's liberated speech about God, his rich metaphorical language which honors no conventions. Jeremiah refuses every reductionism about God who is variously presented as:

a bridegroom now abandoned (2:2)
a fountain of living water (2:13)
better than bridal ornaments (2:32)
a wounded, betrayed father (3:19)[19]

a lion, a wolf, a leopard (5:6)

a civil engineer (5:22)

a man with heart trouble (8:18)

a potter (18:1)

The God rendered here by imaginative poetry is a free, passionate God who presses Israel's speech to its imaginative limit. I suspect that we lose vitality in ministry when our language of God is domesticated and our relation with God is made narrow and predictable. The reduction of metaphor not only abuses the text but betrays the available energy for its present interpretation.

Jeremiah's voice asserts an incredible freedom about God, so that each time he speaks to God or about God, he has the amazing capacity to create a quite new scenario that keeps all parties open and in jeopardy. Predictable language is a measure of a deadened relationship in which address is reduced to slogan and cliché. Vitality of this kind resists every reductionism. The tradition of Jeremiah makes available to us a God who is dangerously on the move in the midst of a specific social crisis.

This poetic articulation of God is an important issue for our own time. Twin temptations beset us in our presentation of God. On the one hand, we may be tempted to a scholastic reductionism about God, so that all things are thought to be settled about God and nothing is left open. On the other hand, we may be tempted to render God only in psychological, personalistic terms so that the terrible sovereignty of God is nullified. Neither way will make the God of the Bible available to us. Both are idols lacking in power and vitality.

The poetic practice of Jeremiah is an invitation to seek for language that is passionate, dangerous, and imaginative enough to make available the passion, danger, and freedom of God who summons us to God's own conflict. It is always a practice of such prophetic poetry to break the conventions in which we habituate God. The dulled God of the conventional religious tradition will never yield energy for ministry. But this poetry gives us hints and permission about bringing this conflict-making God to speech. Otherwise we may miss the conflict which is our poetic, prophetic vocation.

Jeremiah has a sense of the large public issues. He perceives how they relate to pastoral action. His is a pastoral presence of one who genuinely cares for his community. The prophet cares even for the king who did not listen to him, cares enough to speak the dangerous truth. The poet understood that if one tries to care for this people in a protected vacuum without reference to the real life context, one loses vitality because one is engaged in a charade. When one has a "hidden motive for pastoral action,"[20] then one may focus on "the care of souls" without reference to the awesome and ominous events of the world around us. Such pastoral care is finally a lie, and living such a lie will rob us of energy.

1. The overriding historical, theological reality in Jeremiah's perception is that God's people are to be given over into the hand of the Babylonian empire. What a judgment! This threat to Jerusalem is not because of Babylonian expansionism or Babylonian might or power; it is because it is Yahweh's will both for Babylon and for Judah. Thus the text dares to call the despised, feared Nebuchadnezzar "my servant" (25:9; 27:6). Over and over, in unambiguous prose (21:4-7; 17:4; 19:15) and in daring poetry (15:5-9; 12:7-13), Jeremiah has God say, "I am giving you into the hand of Babylon." This was by no means an obvious fact to the contemporaries of Jeremiah. There were surely those who thought the temple would keep folk safe even in the face of political reality (7:4). There were those who looked to Egypt for relief. There were those who, like Hananiah, regarded Babylon as a flash in the pan that would not last (28:2-4). But Jeremiah by shrewdness, by discernment, by revelation, had made this profound decision about the will of God for God's people. Moreover, he believed that there were no decisions of a personal, moral, spiritual, liturgical, political, or strategic kind that could be made without reference to this decision. It is the overriding conviction of his ministry and everything else is judged by that.

Pastoral vitality is related to a concrete sense of what God is doing in the world. If one has not made a bold decision about that, then one must keep juggling and vacillating. That is exhausting and finally robs one of authority and credibility. Of course, Jeremiah could have been wrong, but the community which values the text has judged him to be correct. He read rightly the direction of God's intent.

2. To draw analogies or parallels concerning public issues in our time is inevitably hazardous. The Babylonian reference is not of much

concrete help to us for our own proclamatory work. Indeed it is problematic, because if one is to find parallels, one might conclude that the American community is nearer to the role of mighty, hated Babylon than it is to little Judah. But, if we, like Jeremiah, are to do serious pastoral care, we must ask about the character of such an interpretive decision. I would draw an analogy in our time to that of Jeremiah without too much specificity in this way: Our known world is under judgment and is ending, the known world of moral certitudes, technological superiority, political dominance and economic monopoly. All of the energy used to keep that old imperial world intact is not helpful, is wasted, and is in fact a way of disobedience. Jeremiah articulates that known world now ending in various ways. His articulation includes the end of the temple (chap. 7), the end of the dynasty (22:20), and the reversion of creation to chaos (4:22–26). Each is a metaphor characterizing the nullification of an entire organization of social power and social meaning.

If it is a legitimate move out of Jeremiah into our own circumstance, it cuts underneath our liberal and conservative divisions. And if that is true, then a pastoral model that reassures and provides certitude and tries to keep the old world credible is likely a disservice and a misreading of historical reality. In any case, if we set ourselves against the flow of God's governance of the world, we are sure to be at a loss for energy and credibility. Such false assurances against the direction of God's intent may be paralleled to Jeremiah's false cohorts (cf. 8:8–10).

3. If I were to press the Babylonian connection further, I would appeal to Langdon Gilkey's *The Sacred and the Scientific*.[21] Gilkey argues that the overriding spiritual and cultural fact in our generation is the end of the Enlightenment, which is a model of life concerned for *control through knowledge,* scientific, economic, political, psychological, that is now ending.

Jeremiah's version of the failure of "control through knowledge" is found in his massive critique of prophets (23:9–22), of scribes and wise men (8:8), of priests (2:8). All of the handlers of official knowledge lack the knowledge that gives life (9:3). The leadership is stupid (4:22) and does not know Yahweh, that is, does not have the covenantal discernment that permits well-being. This insight makes us very anxious because we deeply fear loss of control. But loss of control of the known world is what 587 as a metaphor is all about. Vitality in ministry comes in helping people link personal life to the places where God is at work in larger contexts of dismantling. There are no personal issues that are not of a piece with the great public issues. To divide things up into prophetic and pastoral is to betray both. Jeremiah holds them together with his sense about God's governance of the historical process. The "end of the Enlightenment world" is a broad cultural phenomenon, but it impinges directly upon our personal lives even among those who would never think in these large terms. The parallel for ministry, I propose, is this: As God has intended the destruction of the city of Jerusalem, so God may now be discerned as moving against the Enlightenment until it is dismantled.

Jeremiah has a vigorous sense of his own call. He not only has a sense of the one who calls, but he has a sense of what it means to be called. I use the term "call" not in the sense of a datable experience, but as a sense that one's life has a theonomous cast, is deeply referred to the purposes of God, which gives freedom and distance and perspective in relation to all other concerns. Such a call is not an event, but an ongoing dynamic of a growing and powerful claim. One's embrace of a sense of call may mature in time and grow beyond the innocence of the outset. Thus, many scholars suggest that Jer. 1:4-10 is not a report of what happened in the youth of Jeremiah, but it is a reflective statement of authorization much after the fact. Jeremiah 1:5 speaks in some sense of "predestination": "Before you were born . . . from the womb." Surely such a sense of being predestined is a judgment reached only in reflective maturity, not in innocent enthusiasm. So Jeremiah was able to say that he had the freedom and courage to march to a different drummer precisely because his life was defined and shaped by one other than himself, even before he had decided anything. Jeremiah finds the summons of God an irresistible power in his life.

1. "Call" has to do with service to this particular God. "Call" is not simply a formal notion or an energizing experience, but it has substance that relates to the will and purpose of this God. Thus, for Jeremiah the predestination of 1:5 is defined by the commission of

1:10.[22] Jeremiah is formed in the womb in order that he may speak about "tearing down and plucking up," about "planting and building." The call of Jeremiah is not general but is about something very specific. The six verbs in 1:10 concern losing the old world and receiving a new world (see my Introduction); they are about *relinquishing and receiving*. This is the meaning of his call, because that is now the future for his people. The verse (1:10) authorizes a fundamental *displacement* and *discontinuity* which the prophet must bring to speech. Ministry for Jeremiah is helping people make those moves, both of which are weighty moves, surely resisted. The power and authority of v. 6 cannot be taken without the substance and truth of v. 10. An evangelical sense of call concerns the yielding up of our safe world. Jeremiah himself had to make that yielding, even as he called his community to do the same.

2. We need to recognize that such a sense of call in our time is profoundly countercultural, because the primary ideological voices of our time are the voices of autonomy:[23] to do one's own thing, self-actualization, self-assertion, self-fulfillment. The ideology of our time is to propose that one can live "an uncalled life," one not referred to any purpose beyond one's self.[24] It can be argued that the disease of autonomy besets us all, simply because we are modern people.[25] But we should note that the same crisis confronted Jeremiah. After he gives warning to his people, he discerns their stubborn autonomy:

> For long ago you broke your yoke
> and burst your bonds;
> and you said, "I will not serve." (2:20)

But they say, "That is in vain! We will follow our own plans, and will every one act according to the stubbornness of his evil heart." (18:12)

Autonomy is the predictable ground for resisting the truth of a call from outside self.

3. If the ideology of autonomy talks us out of our call as it talked ancient Israel out of its call, we too may settle for idolatries that feel and sound like a call. An idolatrous alternative may take the form of a moral crusade in which we focus on one moral issue to the neglect of everything else. It may take the form of a dogmatic crusade, which is often a disguised form of maintaining monopoly, an ecclesiastical pas-

sion, or an echo of civil religion. These are all diversionary activities to keep from facing the yielding in obedience that belongs to all who are called by this God. All of these alternatives from the perspective of the called Jeremiah are false calls. They are in fact attempts to keep the known world safe, to preclude the dismantling work of Yahweh.

In contrast to all of these self-serving alternatives, Jeremiah understands call to be deeper and more dangerous. The holy purposes of God move in upon and against all of our arrangements. Jeremiah is an example of one who fights the call. This is evident not only in the protest of 1:6 but also in 20:9. Finally, however, this call is embraced by Jeremiah. He would not wish it so. But it is the embrace of the call which unambiguously gives the prophet passion and vitality to do what he must do. He is compelled and will yield. And when he yields, he must face the conflicts that come with his radical call. He must speak of plucking up and tearing down against an ideology that denies discontinuity. He must speak of plenty and building in a context of despair that hopes nothing.

Because his call designed him for conflict, Jeremiah understood there were not any safe places. It is not as though he had his life well put together and then in some phase of it he took on this additional encounter. It is rather that his entire reading of reality put him into the tension under which he seemed to live in all seasons of his life. He understood that conflict, based on call, was the decisive characteristic of his life. "The called life" is a life in process, under way and at risk. We, like Jeremiah, have a yearning for a season of equilibrium, but it is in fact not given. His conflicted life is rooted in his call. So it is for anyone who is summoned by this God to this same obedience.

1. Out from his call, Jeremiah's life moves into a variety of conflicts. The conflict is evident in his quarrel with the kings (22:10–30; 23:1–4). The kings are the bearers of promise, the definers of reality, and holders of decisive power. How strange that Jeremiah was able to speak "truth to power." Thus, he sets up the shattering contrast between the wickedness of King Jehoiakim and his righteous father, Josiah (22:13, 19), arguing that it is only justice that makes real kingship. Any other claim of royalty is false, to be rejected. That same over-againstness is evident in his interaction with Zedekiah. This does

not mean the prophet is personally hostile, as he does make entreaty to this king for his own well-being (37:20–21). But on the main issues he is uncompromising. Zedekiah asks for a word from the Lord (38:18),[26] and receives one. But the announcement is the end of the Judean world of power and well-being, not a word readily received. The most dramatic conflict with the kings is the scene of the burning of the scrolls by Jehoiakim (36:20–26). Even there Jeremiah is undaunted. He commands immediately that another scroll be prepared, to be offered as an alternative to a royal reading of reality (36:28). The narrative shows that the power of the prophet in the conflict with the king is considerable, and not to be lightly dismissed.

That Jeremiah is designed for conflict is also made clear in his interactions with the prophets who mostly were the legitimators of the establishment. He includes the prophets in his general indictment of all the leadership (8:8–13). He offers a massive and programmatic critique of the prophets, concluding that the prophets speak out of their own imagination and not in obedience to Yahweh (23:9–22). More specifically, he engages the words of the prophet Hananiah (28) to show that Hananiah's good word, even if faithful to the tradition, is in fact false.[27] Jeremiah is a free man in his call and will be beholden to none of the standard ideologies of his time, even if they are presented by his adversaries as the word of the Lord.

There is evidence, though not much explicated, that Jeremiah was in conflict with the citizens of his own village, "the men of Anathoth" (11:21–23; perhaps 18:18). We do not know the details about this matter, but at the very least Jeremiah must have been an embarrassment to his own people, perhaps especially to the priestly establishment rooted there. This opposition is not very different from that of the kings and the prophets.

Finally, we observe in the "confessions" that this man designed for conflict is also regularly in conflict with the God who called, authorized, and commissioned him. One might have thought the issue was set so that it would be Jeremiah and Yahweh together against the others. When Jeremiah faces the others, that is how it seems because he claims to be speaking for Yahweh. But on other occasions, perhaps when he is not in a public setting, we see that the conflict in fact sets Yahweh over against Jeremiah. Thus, the conflict is a triangle of

Jeremiah, Yahweh, and the *other leadership.* The demanding and stressful situation of Jeremiah is that he is at odds with the power that might help him both humanly and divinely, both the power of earth and the power of heaven. He is cast in a remarkably lonely role.

2. This problematic of Jeremiah's life causes him to raise the question of theodicy (see especially 12:1).[28] Jeremiah does not even hope for the conflict of human companionship. He understands that is not available to him (15:17), but his hope was that as an obedient servant to Yahweh, he would have access to the fellowship with Yahweh. This also is denied him. He must therefore conclude that God is not equitable in relation to him. The confessions of Jeremiah are not only about a spiritual journey but are a conclusion drawn about the reality of his entire life. His yearning for God is not a pious or mystical quest. It is a court of last resort after every other yearning has failed (18:19). In that painful process Jeremiah learns that his spirituality is not transcendental or romantic or subjective, but it is the serious posing of the justice question which must be done with some nerve. Passion for ministry in Jeremiah is in part because of his readiness to let his *spirituality* take the form of *theodicy.*[29] The conflict ends in the insistence that because he is obedient and faithful, he is entitled to some things and pressed to get them from God, who is not forthcoming. At issue is not only Yahweh's promise but also Jeremiah's claim.

Thus, Jeremiah is aligned against the kings, the prophets, the members of his own town, and finally even God! Most of us would cave in one way or the other. None of us want to be that much at risk, always, incessantly. But Jeremiah is. We may wonder what it does to him. It could drive him to denial, to cynicism, to assimilation; but it does not.

Jeremiah does not wish to be that much at risk. There is a yearning for a season of equilibrium. That is what his confessions ask for. The poems ask for God to let some things be settled on Jeremiah's terms. Jeremiah must struggle in his life of call and conflict. It makes a difference if equilibrium is taken as the norm, as the way life is supposed to be, or if transformative tension is how life really is. He struggles with this, but in the healthy moments of his life he is not ambiguous. He understands and embraces that transformative tension in the life he has been given from God, and he does not regard it as an intrusion in a life that would otherwise be marked by equilibrium. Indeed

Jeremiah knows, in relation to his contemporaries, that the yearning for equilibrium is an idolatrous escape from reality. He knows that his contemporaries cannot finally make such an escape from the living God (10:10), and he comes to know that about himself as well.

3. Not all of us are called to the same vexed life as Jeremiah, but the issue that moves from his ministry to ours is worth pondering. It could be, if these texts have something to teach us, that a life of equilibrium is not in touch with reality, even if we crave such a life of equilibrium. We do so yearn for it, and our popular tradition has taught us to prize it too highly. No one had to ask Jeremiah about yearning for equilibrium. He had been in conflict, with kings, with prophets, with citizens, with God. But that was the nature of his call, to be aligned against the power of earth and the power of heaven. If we do not experience the pain, rage, and dis-ease that goes with such disequilibrium, we may be missing out on our call.

This is not to suggest that we should generate conflict, nor that we should hope for things to be in turmoil. Jeremiah did not need to generate conflict among his fellows. The action of God ending the known world generated enough conflict for all concerned. But it was Jeremiah's sense of God's reality in the midst of the ending that gave Jeremiah vitality, even against God. That vitality put Jeremiah deeply at odds with all the children of equilibrium who did not notice where God was going and who were well defended against noticing. One may, however, conclude that Jeremiah understood that the conflict was generated by the action of God, and so he could live with it and not be immobilized by it.

Jeremiah's language is free, porous, and impressionistic—he is a poet. I have already alluded to this when I mentioned the range of metaphors he uses for God. I judge this to be a most important matter, one that is very difficult for us and one not much noticed. We incline to be reductionist about the prophets and to understand them in ethical categories. Of course the prophets are not strangers to ethical passion. But the overriding reality of the prophets is that they are characteristically poets.[30]

1. Poets have no advice to give people. They only want people to see differently, to re-vision life.[31] They are not coercive. They only try to stimulate, surprise, hint, and give nuance, not more. They cannot do

more, because they are making available a world that does not yet exist beyond their imagination; but their offer of this imaginative world is necessary to give freedom of action. The poets want us to re-experience the present world under a different set of metaphors,[32] and they want us to entertain an alternative world not yet visible.[33] Jeremiah wants his contemporaries to see the world where a decision is already made by Yahweh about the Babylonians. He also wants his fellows to imagine a world where the hurt has turned to healing, but that can only happen if the hurt is properly imagined.

2. Poets speak porously. They use the kind of language that is not exhausted at first hearing. They leave many things open, ambiguous, still to be discerned after more reflection. They do not pretend to know the future, but they offer the present as a shockingly open and ambiguous matter out of which various futures may yet emerge. They do not need to see the end of their words or all the implications before they speak.

There are parts of the Jeremiah tradition that are rather straightforward prose. But there are also poetic elements that push and probe in indirect ways. We will consider only one poem which offers an incredible richness of images:

> At the noise of horseman and archer
>   every city takes to flight;
> they enter the thickets; they climb among rocks;
>   all cities are forsaken,
> and no man dwells in them.
> And you, O desolate one,
>   what do you mean that you dress in scarlet,
> that you deck yourself with ornaments of gold,
>   that you enlarge your eyes with paint?
> In vain you beautify yourself.
>   Your lovers despise you;
>   they seek your life.
> For I heard a cry as of a woman in travail,
>   anguish as of one bringing forth her first child,
> the cry of the daughter of Zion gasping for breath,
>   stretching out her hands,
> "Woe is me! I am fainting before murderers." (4:29–31)

This poem quickly offers us three very different images. The first is about hiding before an invading army (v. 29). The second concerns a prostitute all dressed up (v. 30). The third concerns a woman dying, abandoned in the midst of labor (v. 31). None of the metaphors discloses very clearly the public, discussable issue. Perhaps the first does, because the prophet does want to speak about invasion. Even that image, however, is imaginative. The other two images are more elusive. The images do not describe or teach or compel or instruct. They only push the listener to think further about the world and our posture in it. What is offered is a fantasy about the world under assault, about being vulnerable and lost. The listening community is left to make the linkages to the realities of desperate Jerusalem. The language is open and requires the listener to make some judgments.

3. The purpose of porous language is to leave the poem and the reality to which it points open for the experience of the listener. Poets do indeed trust other people to continue the image, to finish the thought out of their own experience. But that requires the kind of rich metaphorical language that is open and polyvalent. Very often people who hear poets want an explanation, which means to slot the words into categories already predetermined and controlled. Such an act, however, is the death of the poem. If these images from Jeremiah are about the death of Jerusalem, then to have the poem slotted by those who think Jerusalem cannot die is to miss the poem completely. If the words of the poet can be slotted into already existing categories, then one can argue, resist, and reject. Good porous language does not permit itself to be so easily dismissed. It intends to violate and shatter the categories with which the listener operates.

Such an analysis may not strike one as important for our general theme, but I suggest it may be the place where vitality in ministry is most accessible to us. Ministry, as derived from Jeremiah, is as much concerned with the *invitation of imagination* as with *the practice of ethics*. This does not mean ethics is unimportant to Jeremiah or to us. It means rather that we must find a fresh way into the matter. I am increasingly convinced by Paul Ricoeur that people are changed, not by ethical urging but by transformed imagination.[34] Jeremiah's rich imagination intends to challenge the settled givens which make policy too self-confident and unquestioned. Such a social function of poetry is an aspect of the critical study of Jeremiah that is yet to be undertaken, an issue that cannot be reduced to the usual literary analysis of prose and poetry.

In our time one can notice the absence of poetic imagination in some of the religious hucksters who promise certitude by flattening out all the rich metaphors. What Jeremiah understood so powerfully is that he was engaged in a battle for the public imagination of the community.[35] The dominant imagination in Israel had counted heavily on the royal ideology and the claims of the temple. But that claim which had begun in the imagination of David had become establishment ideology.[36] It was an issue whether Jeremiah and his ilk could provide the alternative imagination that would let the painful events of those years be discerned differently. The enormous opposition Jeremiah evoked indicates how profoundly committed his contemporaries were to the maintenance and defense of a certain theological conclusion about the historical process that no longer allowed any imagination.[37]

In our day, many in ministry are caught in bitter exhaustion because people seem so resistant. That resistance, I submit, comes from a frightened, crushed imagination that has been robbed of power precisely because of fear. Indeed, one can note the abysmal lack of imagination in the formation of policy about either international security or domestic economics. We can think of nothing to do except to do more of the same, which generates only more problems and more fear. When we are frightened, we want certitude, not porousness. So the voices of religious certitude and the advocates of political domination seem persuasive. It was so in Jeremiah's time. The religious leadership said, "The temple of the Lord, the temple of the Lord, the temple of the Lord is this" (7:4). The political leadership said, "Peace, Peace," even though there was no peace (6:14; 8:11).

This conflicted man Jeremiah knew one additional thing. He knew that there must be porousness if there is to be life. Without it, life is reduced to the narrowest form of control. Thus the poetry of Jeremiah is an invitation to his contemporaries to experience failed Jerusalem in new ways. It is, however, precisely a new experience of failed Jerusalem that is so mightily resisted.

The practice of such poetic discourse is very difficult. It is difficult because it takes more energy than our conventional prose which is predictable and accepted on all sides. It is difficult, secondly, because it will be very much misunderstood. We are not accustomed to such communication. But the risk must be taken. Jesus' parables stand as witness that the kingdom comes by imagination, by poetic discourse.[38]

Such a way of speech creates vitality in ministry, because it keeps possibility open in the life of the community.[39] Where there is not speech which keeps possibility open, we are left only with necessity. That is what the rulers of this age may want.[40] But that ends in death.

Jeremiah is prepared to join issue around matters of truth and falsehood.[41] Because he is a porous, impressionistic poet, however, it does not follow that he is a relativizer. Jeremiah would have found odd and scandalous our modern notions of individualized truth in which each person is free to hold his or her own perception of truth. He would have found even more odd and scandalous the notion that the pastor or teacher is one who only processes the conversation and manages various "truth claims" upon which the community is deciding. He would have found it offensive to be invited to a "neutral pulpit." But he would also have found it odd and scandalous to practice a truth that was in fact only ideology designed to serve and maintain the status quo, with the effect of protecting people from what is really going on with them. He would have resisted trotting out the banner of truth for every little conviction that might be under discussion.

Jeremiah reserved the question of truth/falsehood for two interrelated matters. First, the issue of truth for Jeremiah concerns *the reality of God.* Vitality in ministry requires reopening the God question. On the whole, liberals believe that to be an unimportant question. Conservatives believe the issue is settled in some catechism formula or some dogmatic conclusion. But Jeremiah conducts his own ministry on the assumption that the God question is open and must be pursued, that it matters decisively as a pastoral agenda and is not settled. If the God question is not seriously pursued, then we have no chance of getting at the *idolatries* in every aspect of life which seem like reasonable facsimiles. In Jeremiah's time the idols took the form of royal propaganda, the false notion that if God is static and tame enough, one can prop up present power arrangements.

The question of God is closely related to the second concern for Jeremiah: *a true or false reading of social reality.* Of course a true or false reading of social reality is derivative from and closely related to the truth or falsity of God. The issue is presented in this way: Is the true God in fact bringing an end to the known world? Who will keep it going in the face of the Babylonian threat? That issue is most clearly put in Jeremiah 27—28, in conflict with Hananiah. In chapter 27, Jeremiah repeatedly makes the same points:

> I have given all these lands into the hands of Nebuchadnezzar. (v. 6)

> Do not listen to your prophets . . . who say, "You shall not serve the king of Babylon." It is a lie. (vv. 9–10)

> Bring your neck under the yoke of the king of Babylon. (v. 12)

> Serve the king of Babylon and live. (v. 17)

> They shall be carried to Babylon and remain there. (v. 22a; au. trans.)

Nothing could be more clear. To be sure, in v. 22 Jeremiah adds an important "until." Then I will bring them back and restore them to this place. But that is remote and not to be counted on now. Whoever regards that restoration as soon is engaging in self-deception.

The issue is, of course, joined in chapter 28. Hananiah regards Yahweh as the sure ally and patron of Jerusalem, and therefore he cannot believe that Yahweh would destroy it. Therefore, the exile into Babylon is momentary and not to be taken with any finality. The point is reiterated in vv. 2-4, 11. The two prophets have different perspectives on historical reality precisely because they have very different discernments of God. Hananiah argued that God would very soon restore the well-being of Jerusalem, that exile is not decisive but only an interlude. In 28:15 Jeremiah responds, "You have made the people trust in a lie." The debate is not only about social reality and social policy. It is about the reality of God, the sovereignty and the freedom of God. Is God an independent reality or simply a derivation from the existence of Jerusalem? The question of truth and falsehood turns on the reality and freedom of God.

There is no doubt that ministry is robbed of vitality and authority by participating in a charade of protecting self and others from the truth of the gospel. There is a kind of conspiracy of deception that keeps the dominant values of our culture credible. There are things that we do better not to speak about. As that happens, we are less and less aware of what is happening to the human spirit and to the human community. We cover over the realities of human hurt and human hope with slogans of mastery, control, and security. Many people want the church to participate in the charade, to sanction it, and to bless it. But such a kept notion of truth makes vitality and authority impossible. Jeremiah, and those who join his ministry, articulate another truth that is less welcome, more dangerous, wrought out of God's pain.

Jeremiah is profoundly a poet of hope. He remembered his full call, so he focused on the four verbs of 1:10, "to pluck up and tear down, to destroy and overthrow." He helped people relinquish a false world that is under threat from God. Critically this means that the greater portion of his work comes from before 587. But Jeremiah remembered his full call. He remembered that 1:10 also said a word about planting and building. Out of that commision of Jeremiah comes his resilient hope. He was able to speak a true word of hope at the point of genuine nullity. Of course there are difficult critical questions, and many scholars would place the hope passages in the tradition of the Deuteronomists, but we are attempting to understand the Jeremiah given us in the text, albeit given us by the Deuteronomists.

The poet has the capacity to speak newness out of nullity. This matters enormously to us, even as it did in the time of Jeremiah. The ideology of our age does not believe in real newness. It does not believe in the possibility of a new Jeremiah, so it must hold desperately to the old one. It does not believe in the resurrection, so it must hold to a messiah who never dies. It does not believe in a God who can work a real newness at the zero point and so it must defend, guard, and protect at all costs the old, which is thought to be the only source of life. To some extent we have all become apostles of continuity, extrapolation, and derivation. Such a view of newness that is not real newness makes us grudging and fearful. It urges us to keep the wagons tightly in a circle. Such a view of the future robs us of vitality because we believe that what we have is the only source of anything in the future.

Jeremiah's vitality comes precisely from his passionate conviction about the power of God to work a newness in the zero hour of loss and exile. Jeremiah does not believe the world is hopelessly closed so that living is only moving the pieces around. Jeremiah believes that God is able to do an utterly new thing which violates our reason, our control, and our despair. Jeremiah bears witness to the work of God, the capacity to bring a newness *ex nihilo*. For that reason loss and emptiness are not the last word.

This remarkable dimension of hope is on the lips of this poet of realistic judgment. Even in his harsh confrontation with Hananiah, in which he insisted on the long-term reality of Babylon, twice he utters this ''until'' of new possibility:

> until the time of his own land comes. (27:7)

> until the day when I give attention to them, says the Lord. Then I will bring them back and restore them to this place. (27:22)

In his word to exiles, after he has admonished getting used to exile (29:5-9), he then moves to announce Yahweh's intention for newness:

> For I know the plans I have for you, says the Lord, plans for welfare and not for evil, to give you a future and a hope. . . . I will be found by you, says the Lord, and I will restore your fortunes and gather you from all the nations and all the places where I have driven you, says the Lord, and I will bring you back to the place from which I sent you into exile. (29:11-14)

God is not simply code language for what is happening anyway. The God of Jeremiah is an independent agent with a plan and intent of his own, which is Israel's only serious hope in exile.

The texts of ''planting and building'' are concentrated in chapters 29—33. They concern return from exile, restoration of destiny, and especially new covenant.[42] What would happen to ministry and to church if the church were the place where there is talk about the newness of God in the midst of the shambles of broken marriages, failed church, diseased society, troubled faith? It becomes not simply a question of rhetoric or of strategy. It is a faith issue in the ministry, whether we are adherents to the resurrection or whether we join the heavy despair. Resurrection faith is not only something for funerals. It is a question of the kind of world that can be spoken by poets in the face of a world that has failed. The alternative to such a dangerous faith is to join in the cover-up. That of course never yields vitality.

Jeremiah's vitality shows up just where one might expect him to falter. He has vitality in the face of a fearful populace that feeds itself on self-deception. Jeremiah's central affirmation is this: Royal definitions of realities which count on the patronage of God are fundamentally false. They block us from seeing how life really is and what God is in fact doing. Jeremiah's vitality comes from a certitude that puts him in deep conflict with conventional definitions of reality. Characteristically for such strange poetry, Jeremiah's word is not a sure doctrine or a new piety, or a reassuring morality or fresh economics. It is an assertion that those who hold on to the false definitions of the life-world are living in falseness that can never yield joy. The evangelical alternative to that is to face the exile, where God will meet this people afresh, perhaps with manna. These very sources of vitality were perceived as subversive. They are the very elements of his work that caused him to be reckoned as a traitor (38:4).

In our own situation there is a growing hunch among many people that our problem is that we cannot have it both ways. We cannot both hold what we have and receive God's new gifts. The "treason" that tells the truth is not about either religious convictions or about political orthodoxies. It is about definitions of reality that touch public life but also cripple personal lives. Jeremiah knew he was destined to a life of terrifying freedom and vitality. For all his resistance to God, Jeremiah could not abandon his vocation of freedom and truth that made possible both *relinquishment* and *receiving*.

Jeremiah's ministry, as mediated to us, is marked by an overriding coherence. There had been disclosed to him the one compelling reality, that God has destined the brutal end of the known world. His energies and imagination were relentlessly devoted to that task, and then to the sequential act of conjuring a new world out of God's powerful promise. He did indeed "will one thing," which caused no end of problems but left him a person of vitality and courage. His very mission designed and destined him for conflict with the rulers of this age, but the risks were clear and he knew why there was conflict. The conflict cut so deep because even the promised solidarity with God was not untroubled. Jeremiah lived into the nullification, but by the power of God and by the courage of his imagination, he did not linger there. He moved on to receive the newness God then promised.

2

"BECAUSE NO ONE CARES"

(JEREMIAH 30:12-17)

Jeremiah lived in a time of turmoil. He believed it was a time of dying. He envisioned the death of a culture, a society, a tradition. He watched his world dying and he felt pain. What pained him even more was the failure of his contemporaries to notice, to care, to acknowledge, or to admit. He could not determine whether they were too stupid to understand, or whether they were so dishonest that they understood but engaged in an enormous cover-up. He could not determine whether it was a grand public deception or a pitiful self-deception. But he watched. The dying seemed so clear, so inexorable. Yet they denied. In different moments, he indicts his people of both stupidity (4:22) and stubbornness (18:12).

The end did come. The grand construct that was Judah did end. It had seemed guaranteed to perpetuity. The dynasty lived under the abiding promise of God. The temple was the sure dwelling of God. The city was not only holy but also impregnable. Yet it ended. Some said the city ended because of the massive power of Babylon. Others judged it was poor defense policy by the crown. Jeremiah watched the ending no one thought would come. He makes a very different judgment from that of the royal establishment. He judges that the holy apparatus has ended because Yahweh, its guarantor, had become its enemy. The end of what was presumed endless had come because God finally will not be mocked. Jeremiah is, like Jesus after him, reduced to weeping over this beloved city, its stupidity and its stubbornness (cf. Luke 13:31-35; 19:41-44).

32

A SEASON OF GRIEF

Jeremiah's testimony is a tale of grief. His poetry becomes, as we shall see, a story of newness acquired the hard way, but not first, not predominantly. The man Jeremiah is a voice of deep grief, one who refuses to be comforted (see Gen. 37:35; Jer. 31:15).[1] The book of Jeremiah is largely given over to this sense of loss. This is a meditation on grief, on the clear recognition of loss. We have learned about death and grief in our personal, relational life—from Granger Westberg[2] and from Elizabeth Kubler-Ross.[3] We have learned that letting go is fundamental to moving on. But we have yet to learn in any way about grief as a public practice, about loss as a societal issue. In Jeremiah's time, as in our own, there is denial and cover-up about the end of the system.[4]

The occasion for grief is the quite public matter of the death of Jeremiah's city, his culture, his value system. It was all in profound danger. It was in danger at a surface level because the Babylonian empire was on the move. Little Judah was helpless. But behind that, the danger came from the covenantal realities of life. The real issues concerned responsiveness to Yahweh, obedience to Torah, care for neighbor. Judah had lost its way. It had forgotten the story of deliverance that Israelites had always told (2:6–7). Now the story seemed remote and unimportant. When the story was forgotten, the claims contained in the story were also forgotten. The yearning of God for fidelity was ignored. The insistence of God on being trusted and obeyed was overlooked as unimportant. Soon after the holiness of God was lost, then the claims of neighborly love were also lost. Inhumanity welled up in crucial places (5:26–28). Instead of compassion there was self-aggrandizement. In place of truth came unprincipled calculation.

Jeremiah watched. He saw clearly and knew that death must come to such a people. He has a vivid imagination. He entertains nightmares which are his very own but of a quite public cast. He dreams—and speaks about the coming of great armies from the north (6:29; 5:15–17; 6:22–26). He senses the wrenching of his stomach (4:19). He has a sense of deep sickness because he sees the sickness of his people (8:18–22). And so he grieves. He grieves the loss.

He listens and he hears ancient mother Rachel crying also (31:15). The old mother must know something. What she knows is that the children are forfeited and the future is gone, thrown away in this mad pursuit of well-being which will not work. Jeremiah keeps listening. He dares to think he hears God cry—with tears like fountains, eyes that run like aqueducts (9:1). Yahweh longs to get away because he is exhausted by this people whom he has treasured (8:19) and pursued, who will not notice (9:2). It is a season of grief for Jeremiah and for the God of Jeremiah. Death is coming. Babylon is on a mission directly from Yahweh. Death is coming. The poet speaks not much of anger, nor of indignation. But the grief of the poet is so deep— because it is happening before their eyes, and they do not notice.

The grief is poignant, because his contemporaries do not notice. They do not notice because they are too busy, too sure, too invested, too ideologically committed. They misread so badly. This holy God whose patience they try, they count on the promises of that very God. The old promises sound to them so sure. Jeremiah thinks he knows better, thinks he knows that the promises are not so unconditional as to preclude the loss and the grief and the death.

But one does not know. So one can hope against grief. One can dismiss the grief as being cowardly, overly sensitive, not tough enough, or just plain disloyal. One can move ahead in brazen show of *hutzpah*. One can. But to do so is a terrible risk, because it requires covering over everything that is wrong.

Jeremiah enters painfully Judah's season of grief. All around him it is a season of cover-up because the grief seems so incongruous with all the market indicators. There is grief and there is cover-up. This grief may produce a season of hope. But not soon. Not quickly. Not easily. Not yet. Real hope comes not in tough-minded histrionics but precisely in, with, and under grief. When there is real hope, it will not be found among his brazen colleagues, who by then will be reduced to muteness. It will be Jeremiah who is the voice of suffered hope. It makes one wonder how such a one could be hopeful. Eventually we realize that nobody else could hope, except for those who grieve. Suffering does produce hope (see Rom. 5:3–5).

In these pages I invite you to Jeremiah's season of grief. This text (30:12–17) proposes to us that there is a dying going on among us. It may not be noticed, but that does not keep it from happening. We may wonder only whether we will notice and join mother Rachel, whether we will engage in cover-up, or join the brazen ones and miss the only serious action in Jerusalem, the only action which permits hope.

NEWNESS OUT OF GRIEF

I want to focus on only one particular text, listen to it, turn it about and be surprised, perhaps transformed by it, hopefully with the life disclosed and news freshly given. The text is Jer. 30:12-17.[5] This text occurs in the powerful poetic unit of chapters 30—31, which contain much of the hope material in the tradition of Jeremiah. Chapters 29—33 all concern hope, but these two chapters are the poetic core. The reference in 30:2 suggests that these two chapters may at one time have been an independent literary unit that circulated separately and only later was joined to the main tradition of Jeremiah. It is disputed among scholars as to whether this is from Jeremiah or is redactional material. The momentum of contemporary scholarship tends to be against regarding these as the words of Jeremiah.[6] I am inclined to take a moderately conservative view which holds that at least the nucleus of this material stems from Jeremiah, though to be precise about particular verses is difficult. If we assume these texts come from Jeremiah, then we are driven to ask the crucial question of how a griever can hope. I submit that the answer to this question is found in the very structure of this particular text, so that in this text we draw closer to our theme topic, how it is that grief can permit newness. If we can probe this particular text with attentiveness, we may have clues to the larger issue of grief and hope.

The key argument that Jeremiah has made against his people is summarized with powerful pathos in 30:12-14. The premise for the entire poem is the diagnosis of v. 12:

> Your hurt is incurable,
> your wound is grievous.

Indeed the case is in fact hopeless, and you are left alone, because all those that had hoped for you have given up their hope:

> There is none to uphold your cause;
> There is no medicine for your wound;
> There is no healing for you. (au. trans.)

The poem begins with abruptness and decisiveness. The poet does not fool around. He insists that his listeners for the moment reread their life through different metaphors.' He will not do a political analysis or an economic assessment. By this metaphor of healing he means to cut underneath such analysis that permits an argument. The metaphor is breathtaking and surely stopped the conversation. The closest we come to that metaphor for public life in our contemporary experience is John Dean's alleged warning to Richard Nixon: "There is a cancer alive in your government."

The poet asks about health. The prophet is a medicine man who knows what makes for healing. I do not know if the poem is intended to shock, but with its unwelcome metaphor of sickness to death it surely did, because Judah had managed to lull itself into reinterpreting symptoms of sickness as marks of health.

The diagnosis continues in v. 14 with two new elements. The first concerns international friends:

> All your lovers have forgotten you.

The metaphor is shifted. Now it is not illness but fickleness. The metaphor seems to derive from Hosea. Judah's "lovers" are alternative security systems and likely refer to political allies. But such allies, with their networks of manipulation, are reduced by the poet and rendered simply as acts of unfaithfulness. Judah lived in a world of massive Babylonian power. The little nations scrambled and postured to fend off the empire. Judah is a party to all of that scrambling. One must, as a small nation, keep alive the pretense of health and effectiveness, or no one will be much interested in a mutual defense pact. The other nations finally have Judah figured out—and it is not good. They had come to understand that Judah's capacity for fidelity is nil. Judah is seen by the other nations to be unreliable, and so their verdict is necessary and not surprising: No one cares for you, no one seeks you out, no one pays any attention. Judah's blind pursuit of self-interest, self-security, self-aggrandizement had made it quite untrustworthy. Now it is left alone, exposed, without resources, unable to cope with the threat, left alone to the moves of the historical process and especially the moves of Babylon. Helplessness is thus added to the problem of sickness.

After the diagnosis in v. 14, the poet has Yahweh give a theological reason for this sorry situation:

> I have dealt you the blow of an enemy.

I have treated you not like a covenant partner, but like an adversary. You have forfeited all special privilege. The reason is neither economic nor political. The metaphor is hardened and the reason for the wound is framed in straight covenant talk:

> because your guilt is great,
> because your sins are flagrant. (30:15)

That is why this is sickness to death. Jeremiah has spent much energy articulating the guilt that is flagrant. It has to do basically with 'azaz, with forsaking, with abandoning first love (2:1-3), with forgetting rootage and reference, with denying heritage, with trading living water for broken cisterns (2:13), with abandoning love like a female camel in heat, ready to copulate with anyone available (2:23-24). Judah has forgotten who she is, a people formed out of Yahweh's love, a people shaped for Yahweh's obedience, a people entrusted with Yahweh's vision of the future. Judah has no other ground for life, no other hope, no reason to be, apart from this vocation. When that is lost, Judah is exposed to every virus, subject to every disease, vulnerable to every deceptive ally. Behind the deadly pathology is none other than Yahweh, who finally has had enough and will take no more.

Verse 15 is a reprise on the main theme, in the form of a scolding: "Why do you whimper over your terminal illness?" (au. trans.) You need not waste your tears here because the judgment is irreversible. That will not change. The reason for the illness, moreover, is clear. There is real guilt. Guilt costs, even to death, when it violates this awesome covenant partner.

Jeremiah speaks not out of indignation but with firmness born out of exasperation. The poet sees the sickness so clearly, grieves the death so passionately. Judah seems not to notice the stench of death in the streets of Jerusalem. This is a people dying, a city on its way to the grave, and Judah has no sense of having lost its way.

By the end of v. 15 we come to a climax and an ending. The rhetoric has wound down. The poet could hardly continue because there seems not much left to say. We are surprised when v. 16 begins with "therefore." The word "therefore" is such a heavy and ominous word for the prophets. Whenever they have God say "therefore," we anticipate yet another threat:

You only have I known of all the families of the earth;
therefore I will punish you for all your inequities. (Amos 3:2)

You build Zion with blood and Jerusalem with wrong,
Therefore Zion will be plowed as a field,
  Jerusalem shall become a heap of ruins. (Mic. 3:12; au. trans.)

There is swearing, lying, killing, stealing, and committing adultery....

> *Therefore* the land mourns . . .
> the beasts of the field, . . .
> the birds of the air, . . .
> the fish of the sea are taken away. (Hos. 4:2–3)

In our text we are at the "therefore." It is enough to make Jeremiah's listeners tremble in anticipation. The rhetoric shocks. As the poet continues, we experience a complete reversal in the rhetoric. He does not say, "Judah will be devoured," but rather something like this:

> Who devours you will be devoured,
> who would exile you will be exiled,
> who would despoil you will be spoiled,
> who preys upon you will be prey.[8] (au. trans.)

The "therefore" of intense judgment has been transposed into an act of protection and solidarity. The very God who raged in vv. 12–15 is now the God who stands as guardian. Babylon or any other hostile agent will have to deal with Yahweh first in order to get at Judah.

The voice of *harsh threat* has inexplicably become the sound of *assurance.* It is done by the poet in one quick rhetorical move. It is a rhetorical move available only to people who follow the contour of the poem carefully. It is only speech, only metaphor, only poem. But everything depends on the poem and the poet, for our worlds come from our words.[9] Our life is fed and shaped by our metaphors. To have our "therefore" of threat transfigured into a "therefore" of solidarity is stunning and decisive.

In, with, and under the poem is the gospel. The gospel given to this terminally ill Judah is that as the poet has reversed the rhetoric, so God has reversed the course of historical judgment. At the point of deep hurt, which is not to be cried over, God has made a new move. It is a move made only in the midst of the candid diagnosis. It is not a part of a cover-up or good news based on denial or escapism. It is not a word spoken by Yahweh in ignorance about the real pathology of Judah. It is rather a word of "second truth" that comes only with and after the first word of truth. It is a word of second possibility as the first possibility of old life is read to its harsh ending.

The God of grief and indignation has, in this rhetorical move, become a powerful advocate. Notice what follows:

> I will return you to health,
> I will heal your wounds. (au. trans.)

The contrast is clear: "I will restore you . . . your pain is incurable." Even if we reverse the sequence: "Your pain is incurable . . . I will restore you," the contrast is still clear. Either way the poem presents a contradiction: "I will heal your wound . . . there is no healing for you." How could it be? It is a miracle wrought by the transformation of God. The incurable is healed. The "no healed" is restored. The change in the hurt could only happen by the change in God.

How is this change in God to be understood? God is not immutable, but God also is not excessively preoccupied with metaphysical freedom. God is a covenant partner who responds in odd and unexpected ways to the reality of the other partner. I suspect the clue to God's change of heart is given us in the last line of v. 17: "because they have called you an outcast. . . ." The nation called Judah an outcast. They noticed that God's people was now in dire straights, obviously having been abandoned. So they mocked and laughed. Do you know where the nations learned such a conclusion? They had heard none other than Yahweh say it: "No one cares for you" (v. 14). Yahweh said those words with some satisfaction, describing Judah's actual historical situation. But now in v. 17, the nations say what Yahweh had previously said. They mocked Judah: Where is your God? Has your God forgotten you? Is God's arm shortened that God cannot save (Isa. 50:2)?

God hears the nations repeat God's own words. Now, on the scornful lips of the mocking nations, the same statement is not acceptable to God. God discovered that what seemed appropriate on God's own lips is now an affront to God's ears. God will not tolerate others speaking of this beloved partner with such cynicism and disdain. God's language in vv. 14–15 seemed ready to abandon Judah to the deathly destiny it so well deserved. But when the echo of God's own words is heard in the voice of mocking, God becomes aware of how deep is God's own hurt, how much God yet cares, how deeply bound in covenant is this God who thought one could walk away in indifference. God finds God's self unable to walk away. The incurable ailment of Judah that is justly deserved now becomes the focus of God's attention, energy, and mercy.

The poem of Jer. 30:12–17 is thus the good news that God has come full circle. The change in God comes to expression in the structure of the poem. The God who was prepared to *abandon* in hostility is the God who *embraces* in passion. As God comes full circle, this beloved people comes full circle *from* terminal illness *to* powerful healing. Or, read historically, this people abandoned to *exile* is now the target of luxuriant *homecoming*. This Judah whose history has ended in hopelessness is a new Judah come back to start over again on a new basis (cf. 23:7–8).

We do not, of course, read this change in God as a statement of cheap grace or easy promise. If we do that, we miss the point of the poetic structure. The poem does not offer one sustained development that may be read straight through from v. 12 to v. 17. That would be easy but false. The message here is not that God always loves and will always love Judah. Rather, this poem discloses the structure of the gospel. Between v. 15 and v. 16 there is a deep abyss. It is the utter break point of Judah's full illness and God's utter alienation.[10] No cheap grace permits Judah or Yahweh to move across the break. The central issue in the Bible is how God or Judah can bridge that break point. I submit that is now our question in the American church, for those who have noticed. It is the question for liberals who do not want to honor the poetry of discontinuity enough. It is the question for conservatives who want to build a bridge out of morality. The question for all of us is how the dread "therefore" of judgment can be transformed. It will not do to minimize the dread of the "therefore" or its judgment, because the break is upon us. The break is real. We are a people at death.

My exposition thus concerns the shape of the gospel in the sixth century B.C.E. and the shape of the gospel as it is offered to us now. It is shaped like a break point of deep hurt, deep illness for Judah, deep alienation for God. Sweet-talk, denial, and surface good news will not permit us to move across the pain that goes with such an ending.

What will permit the move? I think only this: *Only grief permits newness.* It is God's grief that permits the "therefore" to become an act of solidarity. If God had not grieved when hearing the mocking voice of the nations, there would have been no healing. If Jeremiah had not cried his way through chapter 4 and chapter 8, God would not have had a new word to speak in chapters 30—31. If our fathers and mothers had not sat and wept in Babylon by the canals (see Psalm 137 and Lamentations), there could have been no poet to say, "Comfort, comfort my people" (Isa. 40:1). The very structure of the gospel is an argument that pain felt and articulated in God's heart permits new possibilities in the historical process—the good news concerns God's transformed heart.[11] The possibility for Judah, Israel, church, is to participate in God's grief about the terminal illness, to participate so deeply that newness has a chance. The God given us in the poem in vv. 16-17 is a different God from the one who spoke in vv. 12-15. This transformed God is now on the other side of grief, ready now for a newness. This God is chastened, sobered, and wounded and now speaks a newness of power and healing that before had not seemed possible. Except for God's grief, the dread "therefore" might be and remain only judgment. But God grieves and the "therefore" introduces an odd, unexpected newness.

THE OPPONENTS OF GRIEF

This poem, like much caring poetry, is not just addressed into undifferentiated space. It is addressed to real men and real women in real contexts. In the first instance, I want to ask, for whom is this poem intended? But I want to sharpen the question to ask—against whom does this poem speak? Every center of power fears poets, because poets never fight fair. We may ask whom this poem attacks and who would like to silence this poem. After all, this is only a poem. It is not theology or morality or a political proposal. Only a poem, but therefore so dangerous and so powerful. Why did things have to be said so oddly, that the main point is made not by the words but by the form and structure around the transformed "therefore"?

I submit that the enemies of this poem are the managers of the status quo who deceive themselves and others into pretending that there is no illness. They are fascinated with statistics. They are skillful at press conferences. They believe their own propaganda. They imagine that God loves rather than judges, that the Babylonian threat will soon disappear (cf. Jer. 28:2-4), that the economy is almost back to normal, that Judean values will somehow survive, that religion needs to be affirmative, that things will hold together if we all hug each other.

In a word, they believe that grief is treason, that candor about what is underneath only causes failure of nerve and weakens the entire enterprise (38:4). They are into happiness and optimism and well-being. Is this not the indictment Jeremiah makes?

> They, their kings, their princes,
> their priests, and their prophets,
> who say to a tree, "You are my father,"
> and to a stone, "You gave me birth."
> For they have turned their back to me,
> and not their face. (2:26-27; cf. 5:31)

The ideologues around Jeremiah trust excessively in the liturgical formula:

> This is the temple of the Lord, the temple of the Lord, the temple of the Lord. (7:4)

In their own self-interest, they guide policy:

> They have healed the wound of my people lightly,
> saying, "Peace, peace,"
> when there is no peace. (6:14; 8:11)

Such politics seems necessary in order to hold office. Such religion seems necessary to survive, or to "grow." People grow numb and do not notice:

> Thou hast smitten them,
> but they felt no anguish. (5:3)

We call it psychic numbing.

Is it possible that people can be so caught in a bureaucratic ideology, in a self-serving moralism that confuses God and country, in a psychological reductionism, that the hurt must be denied, the anxiety must be covered over, the abyss must be kept invisible? I do not imagine that the people in Jeremiah's time were intentionally evil. They were not "bad people." Not even the priests and not the prophets. Rather, Jeremiah's contemporaries are caught in an ideology of continuity and well-being in which human reality is covered over by slogans. The ideology sponsored by the crown and blessed by the temple is powerful, so that it carries all before it. Juxtaposed to such a powerful combination stands Jeremiah, armed only with a poem to act out his grief. The reality of grief is brought to speech against the slogans of success. The wretchedness of hurt is held up in the face of clichés of security and well-being.

Jeremiah might be only a confused personality, but our tradition affirms that he had a grasp on a truth. He understood in the vexation of his person, that hurt is real, that pain is powerful. If one follows the pain to the "therefore" of God in the poem, God will be transformed into healing power. But if the hurt is covered over and the pain denied, God does not discover how great is his love, how deep her compassion. Where there is no public voice of hurt to express the incongruity, God remains a one-dimensional God of anger and resistance. What is at issue is not whether we shall be crybabies or cranks or soreheads. What is at issue is whether the hurt can be audible and visible enough in the covenantal process to permit God's newness. There are powerful forces at work to stop the poem, because if the poem can be silenced, then the hurt can be exploited, administered, and manipulated. But if the hurt is fully expressed and embraced, it liberates God to heal. Then all of the old power arrangements are jeopardized as the new healing transforms. Nothing but grief could permit newness. Only a poem could bring the grief to notice. The poem is so urgent and so fragile. We cringe from being poets because it puts us next to the "therefore" of God. Between vv. 15 and 16 is a dangerous place for God. Everything depends on being engaged at that point.

THE GRIEF OF JESUS

This one passage (Jer. 30:12–17) should be understood as paradigmatic—as a clue to what occurs in many places. I want to carry this theme of grief/newness one step into the New Testament, to argue that structurally the dialectic of grief and newness is the same in that literature. It is the hurt brought to speech that moves God to newness. Where the grief is silent, the newness does not come and the old order survives another season. But where the grief has its honest say, the news of God's newness is strangely visible. The dramatic counterpart of Jeremiah's grief over failed Jerusalem which must die is in Jesus' weeping over beloved Jerusalem (Luke 13:31–35; 19:41–44). Jesus does not weep in anger or in indignation or with any satisfaction. He weeps in profound grief for this gift of God that has died. "Jerusalem" comes to stand for all the old order of meaning and value and power and coherence, and now it is in death. In Luke 19:41–44, the weeping of Jesus is intentionally linked to the same temple that Jeremiah critiques. In Luke 13, the weeping ends with a hint of a new triumph of Jesus to come. Jesus' ministry is at the pivot point where the old arrangement is in jeopardy. Jesus' main conflict is with the managers of the old order who do not know of its failure and who will do whatever is necessary to keep the grief from becoming visible. For if the grief does not become visible, the charade of the old order can be sustained indefinitely. And then newness will never come.

Two other statements in the Jesus tradition are a study in grief and newness. In the terse, abrasive version of the Beatitudes in Luke 6:21, 25, Jesus says:

> Blessed are you that weep now, for you shall laugh, . . . Woe to you that laugh now, for you shall mourn and weep.

The Beatitudes are a study of two ages, the present age and the age to come.[12] They ponder how one can move into the gifts of the new age of the gospel. They take the *form* of good advice, but the *substance* contradicts the form. The "advice" given contradicts all conventional teaching. Weep for the "now" that is dying.[13] If one weeps its death, one will be freed for the newness that God is giving. The weeping is to face reality and then to relinquish it. Harsh judgment is the alternative to grief. Those who laugh now are the ones who do not discern the death, who crave the way things are, who are too invested and enamored of the present arrangements, that is, they love the corpse of the old age (cf. Amos 6:6). For those who do not notice the sickness to death, the future that God will give is a threat and a burden. One cannot both love the old and receive the new. One must choose. Jesus' disciples are those who are able to relinquish present arrangements for the sake of the new gifts of the coming age.

The same juxtaposition and the same problematic choice are presented in the Fourth Gospel, in the Farewell Discourse:

> Truly, truly, I say to you, you will weep and lament, but the world will rejoice; you will be sorrowful, but your sorrow will turn into joy.

As the metaphor continues it presents the sorrow like the pain of a woman in labor:

> When she is delivered of the child, she no longer remembers the anguish, for joy that a child is born into the world. So you have sorrow now, but I will see you again and your hearts will rejoice, and no one will take your joy from you. (John 16:20–22)

The text is called the Farewell Discourse, but it is a *farewell* in *anticipation*. The deep farewell is not to Jesus but to the old world that is under judgment. The affirmation is structured much like the assertion in Luke 6. The disciples are to weep the incurable wound of the present age, even while the world celebrates its pseudo-health in its blindness. The time is soon, says the gospel, for the birth of newness. Then the joy will be staggering. It will be the healing of the incurable wound. But the coming joy depends on the present grief. The new gift is premised on the relinquishment. The sorrow of death permits the joy of new birth. But the new birth "from above" and the rush of the spirit only appears in the hurt and loss of the old dying (John 3:3–15).

It does not surprise us that as Jeremiah was dismissed as a traitor;[14] so Jesus was crucified as a threat. If the healing comes only when the wound is acknowledged, if the new comes only in the presence of explicit grief, then new possibility turns up only in the candor of loss. When life has become a massive denial, there is too much at stake and the new possibility, the new age, the new community cannot be risked.

A SEASON OF TRANSITION

I believe that we are in a season of transition, when we are watching the collapse of the world as we have known it. The political forms and economic modes of the past are increasingly ineffective. The value system and the shapes of knowledge through which we have controlled life are now in great jeopardy. One can paint the picture in very large scope, but the issues do not present themselves to pastors as global issues. They appear as local, even personal, issues, but they are nonetheless pieces of a very large picture. When the fear and anger are immediate and acute, we do not stop to notice how much our own crisis is a part of the larger one, but it is.

When such a massive threat is under way, so comprehensive in scope, so acute in personal hurt, frenzied, dangerous activity takes place. Such activity runs from arms stockpiling to frantic self-fulfillment to oppressive conformity. All of these are attempts to hold the world together enough to maintain our dignity, our worth, our sanity, and probably our advantage. I believe these attempts can be identified among conservatives (including theological conservatives) who want to stop the change by formulae of authority and conformity. I believe these attempts can be identified among liberals (including theological liberals) who want to keep power in place because liberals have had a good season and still trust the worldly knowledge of the social sciences to keep us human and to keep us safe. The voices of newly revived conservatism and responsible liberalism are important. Both voices have something to tell us.[15]

Neither voice, however, touches the issue of the death of the beloved city that must be grieved. Indeed, one can argue that the polarities in our society are a game on which we have agreed in order to keep us busy, so that we do not notice. Powerful vested interests are at work, perhaps mostly unwittingly, to keep the grief from notice. In one way or another, we believe the ideology of our party, our caucus, our nation, our class, because ideology serves as a hedge against a serious diagnosis. If one denies serious illness, then there is no need for the diagnosis. There is then no cause to weep over the city. There is no call for such poignant poetry. But if the city is dying, if the old order is failing, if the poet has diagnosed rightly, then the grief is urgent. It is a personal grief. It is a quite public grief. It is facing our true situation, in which living waters have been rejected and we are left with broken cisterns (2:13), in which all our lovers despise us (30:14), in which we are like restive camels in heat (2:23-34). All the metaphors mediate our broken, beaten fickleness. The news is that God enters the broken, beaten fickleness.

In God's attentive pain, healing happens. Newness comes. Possibilities are presented. But it all depends on being present with God in the hurt, which is incurable until God's hint of healing is offered. We wait, along with the poet, to see what the tone of the next "therefore" will be.

PART 2

ONLY HOLINESS
GIVES HOPE

3

EZEKIEL—TOUGH AND SUBMISSIVE

ELIE WIESEL TELLS a Hasidic story of rabbis who debate and dispute with God over the destruction of God's people. They challenge God, scold, berate, reprimand God in an abrasive fashion, surely beyond propriety and in violation of normal piety. After this has gone on a while, surely longer than God would wish, one rabbi in the discussion reminds the others that it is time for prayer. The rabbis leave off their abrasive argument with God, don their prayer shawls and bow down in reverence and devotion before the Holy One.[1]

That, I take, is what it means to be tough and submissive. We are mostly inclined to be submissive, certainly before God and mostly before human authority. That is the nature of conventional Christian piety. We are mostly nurtured in docility.[2] In such a posture, toughness is treated as irreverence, disrespect, and blasphemy. Or conversely, there may come those break points in one's life and faith where one is not all such trusting submissiveness. We become tough and abrasive, perhaps never to come "home" again. Then there is toughness without submissiveness. It often happens that these two postures are seen as mutually exclusive. Either we will *dispute* or we will *bow down,* but we do not know how to do both in the same life. To be tough and submissive, to be prepared for dispute and for bowing down, is an invitation to a free life with God. This life was understood by the rabbis, who never tried to slot things or reduce life with God to a system but who kept a full life open with God. It is that capacity to be open in many postures with God that leads to vitality in faith.

A DANGEROUS MINISTRY

As that invitation is true with God, so that same invitation may be true in our human relations. Those in ministry have a terrible temptation to take responsibility for others, to do for others what they will not do for themselves. We have a difficult time having enough freedom to disengage ourselves, to let others be free when they are wrong, to let others be free to fail, even when they are surely headed for destruction. Our study suggests that a ministry of vitality requires that we be deeply concerned for and utterly free from other people. We incline to think these are mutually exclusive postures, but it is the capacity to practice both that gives us energy for vocation.

Our study of Ezekiel thus begins in this correlation of our two relationships:

With God: to be tough and submissive, able to dispute and ready to bow down.

With human persons: to be deeply concerned for and utterly free from.

Such correlations toward heaven and toward earth lead one to ask: What kind of boundaries and limitations operate in ministry when we cannot get God or the other people to "act right"?

I pose these questions around the ministry of Ezekiel. Ezekiel is a younger contemporary of Jeremiah. The issues thus are much the same for him as for Jeremiah. The two of them are the only ones we know about who ministered across the discontinuity, that is, before and after 587. While the issues are the same for both prophets, their respective presentations of the issues and their responses to them are very different. Ezekiel, unlike Jeremiah, is a priest, and everything is perceived in a priestly idiom. Popular interpretation tends to dismiss Ezekiel as "bizarre." But Ezekiel may be exactly the right text for such a "bizarre" time as ours.

The priestly cast of issues in Ezekiel may also be pertinent for us, because those engaged in ministry in our society are cast in the role of priests, a role often not understood or easily embraced in conventional

Protestantism. My sense is that the priestly function, especially in the free church traditions, is usually articulated in other idioms, so that the central priestly reality of our life is largely unnoticed, unacknowledged, and unexpressed.[3] If anything, Ezekiel's priestly perception of reality caused him to make a deeper, more anguished assessment of his situation than even Jeremiah did. It is clear that priestly sensitivities are essential in response to some crucial dimensions of religious life.

We begin our exploration of Ezekiel with some comments about the nature of the material.[4] As in the case of Jeremiah, we shall be concerned with the material as it now stands. We are not interested in "historical" questions of Ezekiel but will be concerned with the "canonical Ezekiel."[5] Unlike the book of Jeremiah, the book of Ezekiel has been subjected to symmetrical and clear editing. As a result, the book of Ezekiel falls nicely into two main elements:

Chapters 1—24 are a comment on the preexilic period, which for Ezekiel was limited to the six years, 593–587. Set in a preexilic context, these texts maintain a massive critique of Jerusalem, announcing that it will be destroyed and that God's presence will depart the profaned city. The purpose of this text, I submit, is to *relinquish* the old city that is now gone.

Chapters 33—48 are post-587, which for Ezekiel means 587–571.[6] These are mostly statements of hope and new possibility, helping the people in exile to *receive* the newness of God and act on the new historical possibilities now being made available. These chapters contain some of the most remarkable statements of hope available in the Bible.

Without greater refinement, this is an adequate beginning point for our understanding of the structure of the argument made by the Ezekiel tradition. We may safely ignore the complex questions of layers of editing, as well as the historical questions about the person of Ezekiel. In this broad outline, it is clear that the double agenda of *relinquishment* and *receiving,* of judgment and newness, is the same as in Jeremiah, only here it is much more clearly articulated. The priestly office consists in helping people to face the death already decided upon and to receive new life that comes in after the death.

We will look first at Ezekiel's toughness in his understanding of God, his sense of ethical demand, and his harsh rendering of the tradition. Then we will consider dimensions of submission in the tradition of Ezekiel.

A GOD NOT USEFUL

Ezekiel bears witness to a God who is free, transcendent, and other. I have used the adjective "robust" for Jeremiah. Perhaps the same word could be used here for the God of Ezekiel, but I would not present it so. Jeremiah's robust God is one with whom one can engage and struggle. That tends not to be the case here. Rather Ezekiel stands and watches at a distance, for this is God so utterly *holy* as to be mostly unapproachable. The abominations (8:9, 13) are a profound affront to Yahweh. This way of delineating God is not congenial to our more liberal co-opting of the prophetic tradition. In some ways, unsettling as it is, this view of God is freeing, because it asserts that all human efforts at being right with God and gaining admission to God's presence are so dwarfed as to be irrelevant. The initiative for the relationship is held so closely by God as to discourage human possibility or even human anxiety about possibility.

The key to Ezekiel's proclamation of God is this: *God will not be mocked.* God will not be presumed upon, trivialized, taken for granted, or drawn too close. God takes being God with utmost seriousness and will not be caught in any partisan alliance or any efforts at use. God will not be pressed into the service of any other cause, no matter how noble or compelling. This is an important point for us in ministry as the known world of the Western Enlightenment collapses, for we have arrived at a view of God which is essentially utilitarian. We use God either in conservative fashion to buttress morality and the American way of life or in liberal fashion to provide motivation for social change of various ideological kinds. In the tradition of Ezekiel, against such exploitations, one must talk not even about God's will but about God's person, who is first of all not even to be obeyed but to be honored, glorified, adored, and feared.

In our culture we tend not to acknowledge the reality of God to be so unencumbered as it is here portrayed. Everything among us is reduced to commodity.[7] If something or someone does not have usefulness, that thing can then be safely ignored and forgotten. Surely it is so for those in ministry who tend to have God become an agent and function of the church. The urge to press God toward our need is likely to become even more pronounced when we are caught in anxiety about survival, either of church or social institution or cultural value. In Ezekiel, God is not for us as much as God is for God's self. God refuses to stay where God is not honored (8:6). In our culture, however, such a faith feels either like an unnecessary luxury or an outmoded notion. We build low-roofed churches which foster horizontal fellowship but which have brought the sky down to human proportion.

On the whole, the words of Ezekiel are words of toughness. It is announced that God's glory, God's sovereign presence, will depart (9:3; 10:15–22). God is leaving, is terminating his commitment to his holy city, to our known and previous world. God is not greatly in grief about this departure. Indeed God's departure is coupled with a massive judgment and slaughter of those who have excessively presumed upon God (9:5–6, 9–10). God is, so says Ezekiel, free and can walk away from it all. God cares for God's self and is not trapped in this oriental village called Jerusalem. Indeed God is not trapped in any of the places which have been prepared to house God.

This articulation of God's glory and God's departure is a way to help people think through the absence of God and the conditions under which God will stay or leave. God has no manipulable commitment to any of our structured worlds. It is this conviction which gives the ground for the powerful vision of the wheels at the beginning of Ezekiel (1:4–28), wheels within wheels within wheels. The language is hardly adequate to what Ezekiel has seen or what he wants to say. It concerns the departure of God, God's decision to evacuate in God's freedom and God's holiness. In that moment of departure, God gives no second thought to the place or the people who are left behind. They are no part of God's serious concern. They do not count. The God of Ezekiel is mobile and will not be contained in any of the packages available. God's glory is never reduced or captured. God is not only free, but God is also tough and ruthless. God has the will to leave and not look back.

Certain things follow from this vision of God in terms of vitality for ministry. This portrayal of God suggests that the ministers of this God might learn from the freedom and will of God to maintain some freedom and distance in the daily life of their ministries. Ministry has become exceedingly utilitarian. All of us are too busy being useful. The more there is worry about professional and institutional survival, the more useful we seek to be. Indeed our usefulness at times overrides our ministry, even though much of our usefulness is only related remotely to the reality of ministry. Such an effort at usefulness may rob us of vitality. God refuses to be useful. God's ministers might ask about the temptation to excessive usefulness when the call may in fact be to study and witness to the *unencumbered holiness of God* that places everything on the human side of reality in jeopardy. Such a notion of ministry is frightening. If this, though, is who God is, it could also be a notion of ministry that is energizing and authorizing. Ezekiel did understand that the holiness of God is a reality that jeopardizes. God is not harnessed nor are the ministries of this God finally utilitarian.

THE WEIGHTY IMPERATIVE OF HOLINESS

Of course Ezekiel was not myopic. He understood that God's holiness is not only religious awe,[8] but God's holiness translates into a *summons to righteousness*. Thus the tradition is a call to repentance (14:6). This linkage between holiness and righteousness is a difficult point. If holiness is understood without righteousness, it can be only a religious preoccupation. However, if there is only righteousness without holiness, it quickly becomes moralism and legalism. But here they are together. Because God is free on God's throne (chaps. 1—3), human life on earth must be ordered differently (chaps. 8, 14). The voice of this ethical insistence, however, is not utilitarian. It is not argued that one who is righteous will succeed or prosper or be happy. It is only argued that the ethical imperative follows from the theological vision. The ethical urging of Ezekiel, therefore, is not terribly accommodating; it is rather a truth-telling of things that make for life. Much loss of vitality in ministry is because of the forfeiture of the office of ethical teacher that derives from the reality of God's holiness.

Ezekiel 18 is a marvelous and central summary of what God's holiness requires on earth. It is a catalogue of righteousness:[9]

1. a warning about *idolatry*, v. 6a
2. a warning on *sexual and marital responsibility*, v. 6b
3. a warning on *economic responsibility*, vv. 7–8a

All three items require comment. Idolatry does not have to do with plastic pieces on dashboards but with ideological commitments which assign our deep loyalties to matters of vested interest. It is now asserted by many critics of religion that the problem of our time is not atheism but idolatry.[10] The issue is not that we are nonbelievers but that our belief is assigned to unworthy and unworkable objects. It was the same in Ezekiel's time. The catalogue of chapter 18 is horrendous. What Ezekiel found in Jerusalem was a widespread practice of idolatry, which he regards as an abomination. Such idolatries are attempts, misguided attempts, to secure the city by trust in other gods because the terms of security from Yahweh are too costly.

Serious ministry as embodied in Ezekiel requires profound ethical commitment, but it requires an ethical commitment that is not reduced to a pet project. The juxtaposition of *sexual morality* and *economic justice* in chapter 18 is one that requires serious reflection. It is as though Ezekiel anticipates the critical reflection of Karl Marx and Sigmund Freud and understands how closely related to each other they are. The economic issues concern the unmasking of vested interests; the sexual agenda has to do with repression and with libertinism. This twofold agenda rooted in the issue of idolatry is precisely to the point of our own situation. The catalogue of righteousness in Ezekiel 18 has enough of a sexual agenda to satisfy any conservative who is worried about permissiveness. It has enough of an economic agenda for any liberal who is preoccupied with such public questions. The wonder of the statement is that they are there together. None of us may pick an item we prefer to the neglect of the others. The holy God intends that the two key "neighbor questions" (sexuality and economics) be sorted out on the basis of a right settlement of the God issue. Both issues are related to God's sovereignty and the distortion of idolatry.

The holy city must "turn" if it wants to live (3:19; 18:30–32). Otherwise, the holiness of God will let even treasured Jerusalem float away into oblivion without a tear. There are not enough claims held by Jerusalem to guarantee anything against the holiness of God. Indeed, Jerusalem has forfeited any claim it might have had. All those old Zion traditions are now null and void, and there is left only the righteous will of the holy God.[11]

Concerning the righteousness of God which is derived from the holiness of God, one other text may be mentioned. I refer to the most interesting use of a metaphor of Sodom (16:46-50). It is, of course, well known that the Sodom story in Genesis 19 appears to be about some perverse sexual act, perhaps homosexuality. Like every good poet who speaks the mind of God, Ezekiel handles this particular narrative and metaphor with remarkable imagination. Thus in Ezekiel 16:49 the unrighteousness of Sodom is characterized in a quite new way:

> She had pride, surfeit of food and prosperous ease, but did not aid the poor and needy. (au. trans.)

It is not necessary to adjudicate the claims of sexuality and economics to determine which may be the more crucial demeanor of righteousness. For Ezekiel, both sexuality and economics are aspects of the life of Judah that are askew and that will bring death. They are issues that will cause the absence of God, because God will not be mocked. It is worth noting, however, that in this particular case the prophet translates the metaphor of Sodom in a breathtaking way toward economic issues. This is all the more remarkable when he has spoken extensively about lewdness and abomination in earlier settings. The texts indicate that part of the vitality of his ministry is that Ezekiel had a clear sense of the ways in which the holiness of God was at issue in questions of righteousness and justice.

THE GREAT MISMATCH

Ezekiel has vitality for his ministry because he is able to discern the enormous mismatch between the *disinterested holiness* of God and the *utilitarian unrighteousness* of Israel. It is that mismatch which he judges to be the overriding truth of his ministry. Ezekiel's statement of that mismatch is not intended as scolding, though some of his contemporaries may have thought it was. Nor is his urging reduced to moralism. Ezekiel does not take his stand on the issue of "naughtiness'' but on the holiness of God. The mismatch is traced out in great detail, especially in chapters 7—8.

Chapter 7 is a dreadful statement of judgment. The basis of the judgment is not greatly explicated in this chapter. It is because of abominations (vv. 3, 4, 9), iniquity (v. 19), and detestable things (v. 20). The specific hints of what is wrong include injustice (v. 10) and violence (vv. 11, 23). The text is massive in its statement of judgment. It is a redundant announcement of "the end" (vv. 2, 3, 6) and of "the day" (vv. 7, 10), which will lead to the standard curses of sword, pestilence, and famine (v. 15).

The prophet takes us on a tour of the temple (in chapter 8) and shows us the shameless way in which one can observe in the very temple of Jerusalem ritual activity aimed at the God Tammuz (8:14). His consternation is expressed in the heavy and repeated word "abomination." He knows the mismatch is intolerable and can only lead to disarray.

What is most remarkable is the statement of 8:6 that Yahweh is driven from the temple. That is, Yahweh cannot and will not stay in the midst of such contamination. Ritual uncleanness is incompatible with God's holiness. The incongruity between uncleanness and holiness leads inescapably to God's departure and absence. The priestly symbol system has as its major responsibility to sort out what is clean and unclean (cf. Hag. 2:12–14), so that God's presence is not jeopardized. But the priests indicted by Ezekiel have failed (22:26). The mismatch and incongruity have gone unnoticed in Judah, but for that reason are not exempted from severe cost.

It is not obvious how we should translate that overriding sense of mismatch, but some lines of interpretation toward our own situation may be suggested. In my judgment, mainline churches use too much energy dividing things up along the lines of liberalism and conservatism. The old distinctions between liberal and conservative pale in importance when we consider the reality of God's holiness and the community's unrighteousness. I have already alluded to liberals and conservatives, but in each case my reference has been to insist that both liberals and conservatives are caught in the same cultural realities and that the distinctions between them are in fact irrelevant and obsolete. Such a labeling is not helpful because when we are honest and not partisan, we share a sense, an overpowering sense, of the mismatch in our world between the God whom we profess, toward whom we are ordained, and the actual reality of our world. That mismatch is covered over by our various practices of utilitarianism. Pastors who have eyes to see, see the mismatch in our concern with modern ways of death, in marriages that are without resource, in children who are confused, in affluence that seduces, in inhumanity to people and exploitation of land that have become policy, in the arms race that will destroy us internally before we ever use the weapons. This is not simply an inventory of social issues. It is rather an indicator of the dimensions of the mismatch between us and the holiness of God. When we grow partisan or indifferent, we are insensitive to the mismatch.

That mismatch, that incongruity, is both the substance and the context of our ministry. Were we to face that, we would indeed have vitality, for we would have an urgent preoccupation that would keep us free of the triviality of being useful. This does not, of course, mean that we leave off caring for people or maintaining institutions, but it could suggest the kind of care which is appropriate, the kind of institutions we must reform. I submit that the pastoral care practiced by Ezekiel was precisely to guide people into an awareness of the mismatch so that new decisions could be made appropriate to Israel's actual situation.

THE SUBVERSIVE TRADITIONALIST

Ezekiel is an imaginative practitioner of the root tradition of Israel. He is not a rootless radical who suddenly appears on the scene. It is not as though he is a freshly formed subversive. Ezekiel 16, 20, 23 show that he knew the traditions of his people well.[12] He had in fact thought long about the tradition. He knows and affirms the tradition which is rooted in the oldest credo recitals,[13] but he rereads the tradition in light of his own incongruous situation. As he rereads the credo, he inverts Israel's memory. What had been a recital of God's gifts and interventions now becomes a recital of Israel's abuses and abominations. Even more than Jeremiah did, Ezekiel argues that Israel did not suddenly fall into this mismatch. Israel has been on its way to this mismatch for a very long time, since the beginning of its history, which is part and parcel of a history of harlotry.

Two points may be learned here about the relation between tradition and vitality for ministry. First, the tradition *must be taken seriously*. That in itself is crucial in a society that suffers from amnesia, that is tempted to absolutize the present and tends to dismiss what is past. It is clear that Ezekiel's community had amnesia (cf. Jer. 2:6-8). At every level, ritual and ethical, they had forgotten their identity. And their identity was lost because they had forgotten the classic story of faith. So, for example, Ezekiel 16 presents that whole memory under a most remarkable metaphor of adoption and love, betrayal and alienation. Second, it means that the tradition *must be taken critically*. It should not be taken simply in its obvious or familiar reading. It should not be accepted as it is officially told, because official readings of the tradition tend to be tendentious and ideological. Rather, to read the tradition critically means that the tradition must be reread under the pressure of the mismatch and the incongruity that may bring death.

If perchance Israel did remember the credo recital, it was likely a "whitewash" (cf. 13:11), to present the history of covenant as a happy relationship between a gracious God and an obedient people. Every community tends to be selected in the most positive sense, so that the very recital becomes a systematic distortion.

But Ezekiel reads it another way. This is not a history of a working relationship but a history of an ongoing violation. God's graciousness is articulated in 16:6-14. In v. 15, however, everything is changed. That history is now seen to be a history of misplaced trust (v. 15), harlotry (vv. 22, 26), and insatiable appetite (v. 28), acted out in the most lewd and shocking ways. The prophet is remarkable in this invention of new metaphors for the sake of a radical rereading.

The tradition must be reread to see how and in what ways this mismatch has become the controlling fact or reality. Such a rereading of the memory is, of course, subversive, because it means we discover things about our memory that we have not noticed or have chosen to suppress. This is what Ezekiel does in the long recitals of 16, 20, and 23.

The same rereading is beginning to happen in our contemporary society. Thus, we are noticing the dimension of anti-Semitism in such places as the works of Martin Luther. At many points the rereading begins to expose racism and sexism, which may well be the unwitting precursors of the nuclearism that now destroys us. The rereading lets us see that our history is not all white and male, not all honorable and noble and triumphant. We are beginning to recover the names of women who have been decisive, the names of blacks whom we thought had no "recorded glory."[14] We are beginning to see that some of the important history is written "from underneath" by people whose names have been nullified. Then we notice that the alleged history-makers have sometimes not been history-makers but have been primarily "history preventers."[15] If we are to have vitality for the truth entrusted to us, we, like Ezekiel, will have to work in the tradition much more carefully, so that we are not simply making *ad hoc* observations or reiterating ideological bad habits.

THE SUBMISSIVENESS OF EZEKIEL

We have thus far been speaking about Ezekiel's toughness. He is indeed relentless. He is relentless about the holiness of God, about the requirements of righteousness, about the mismatch between holiness and unrighteousness, about the rereading of the memory as a memory of disobedience. In all of these motifs, one can scarcely detect a trace of pathos, pity, or compassion. Indeed, he is instructed to be ruthless and relentless: "Your eyes shall not spare, and you shall show no pity" (7:4, 9; 9:5).

I want now to comment on the *submissiveness* of Ezekiel. Even in his submissiveness, the prophet is not mellow or romantic. But he does know that as there is "a time to speak," so there is "a time to keep silence" (Eccles. 3:7). The prophet knows he is mandated to speak clearly on behalf of the holiness of God. He is willing to do that at some risk, and he does not flinch from it (cf. 2:4–7).

But he also knows that when his speaking is finished, it is time to desist and leave the decisions to be made by those addressed. Even this most relentless prophet finds a limit to his call and his responsibility beyond which he is not expected to go. That limit to his responsibility is important for two reasons. First, it is important because Ezekiel is not called to be destroyed by his passion. There is a boundary to the cost that he must pay. (In this regard he may be a bit better protected than was Jeremiah, who sensed no such protective limit.) Second, the limit is important, for it reminds Ezekiel that finally the mismatch is not his personal responsibility. It is God's issue, and we are not finally set in God's place. We do not have to do God's work. Ultimately, the mismatch is not our problem. Perhaps it is precisely Ezekiel's high view of God that lets him accept a limit on his own responsibility.

Two rather remarkable facets of submissiveness protect Ezekiel from his call to toughness. The first is seen in 3:16–21. In the fashion typical of Ezekiel, the mandate is wonderfully symmetrical. He is identified as a watchman, one designated by God to warn the community of approaching danger.[16] This he does. He is charged by God to be a faithful watchman. Ezekiel must warn Judah, but that is the full extent of his responsibility. He need not do more than warn them: So if you warn them, and they do not listen, it is not your problem. On the other hand, if you do not warn them, and they die, it is your problem.

He is given a two-pronged message. On the one hand, if the analysis of the mismatch is correct, it means that the central pastoral office is to *make people aware*. There is nothing more important than this, and no other form of usefulness is a substitute. On the other hand, however, there is good news for the prophet. You do not need to answer for them. You do not have to be the church. You do not need to be the American government. You do not have to accept culpability for those acts that are outside the reach of your own life. You do not need to repent for the others, because you cannot. Submission may not be the right word for this, but it feels like submission. There is no final toughness here, but a readiness to let God be God, not to displace God, not to displace neighbor, but to tell the truth and then to trust the process of truth to determine the outcome. But such submission does not short the circuit—the prophet must tell the truth.

This text set right at the beginning of Ezekiel (3:16–21), just after the initial vision, is matched in the second half of the book by another watchman text in 33:7–11. If, as seems reasonable, chapters 25—32 are set aside as different material, then this second text is also set precisely at the beginning of the unit of chapters 33—48. This means, as the Book of Ezekiel is now shaped, this is the first text of the second half of the book. This text (33:7–11) is placed at the very beginning of the block of material presented as hope passages, conventionally dated just after 587. The same point is made here as in 3:16–21.

Ezekiel 33:7–11 sounds as if it is a last-minute skirmish between Ezekiel and his contemporaries, one last exploration of ways to save the city. Ezekiel may be tempted to such pragmatism, but the word of the Lord is that he is not called to such utility. His task is simply to warn, not to figure out ways to save the city. He is clear in the midst of his relentlessness about what he is charged to do and not to do. He must not do less, but also he need not do more. He must let God have God's relentless way. In the drivenness and busyness of ministry, this could be a good word. Ezekiel helps to focus on the essentials. Here the single essential is to be sure that people are clear about the mismatch and the deathliness produced by the mismatch. That is enough of a task, but it is not endlessly exhausting. Passion and energy for ministry may be helped if one has a clear sense of the parameters of one's calling.

A second set of texts speak about Ezekiel's submission, even if it is not a willing submission. These texts are closely related to those concerning his role as watchman that we have just considered. In 3:24, just after the watchman passage and right at the beginning of the pre-exilic material, God tells Ezekiel,

> Go, shut yourself within your house. And you, O son of man, behold, cords will be placed upon you, and you shall be bound with them, so that you cannot go out among the people; and I will make your tongue cleave to the roof of your mouth, so that you shall be dumb and unable to reprove them; for they are a rebellious house. But when I speak with you, I will open your mouth, and you shall say to them, "Thus says the Lord God"; he that will hear, let him hear; and he that will refuse to hear, let him refuse; for they are a rebellious house. (3:24–27)

Ezekiel may want to speak more, but he is required by God not to speak. He is not permitted to speak a new word. He is not permitted to warn, to offer advice, or to offer assurance. Ezekiel must submit to the withdrawal of the word of Yahweh from the people. Where the word is withdrawn, the people cannot long survive. It is as though God were saying, "I know you want to say more things to them, either in your anger with them or in your pity for them, but you cannot. You have told them the truth. Now you must let it go at that."[17] Ezekiel is no longer permitted toughness with God toward Judah. The initiative is taken from him. There are profound critical problems in knowing what this prohibition from God means. I submit, however, that such a mandate to silence could give vitality for ministry. It makes clear what the call is. There are limits. There is a point when enough is enough.[18]

There is a return to the motif of silence in 24:16–24, the very last text in the first half of the book. As the Book of Ezekiel is now arranged, this is the last text in the preexilic literature, the last word before 587. The literature and the speech of Ezekiel are drawn to a close in silence as there is now a move to destruction and exile. The word of Ezekiel is the same, only now much more personal:

> Sigh, but not aloud. Make no mourning for the dead. . . . And the people said, "Will you not tell us what these things mean for us, that you are acting this way?" (au. trans.)

The prophet can only respond, "God told me to do so, because God will now profane the temple." The presence is gone. The word is gone. All is lost. Judah is hopeless. The silence is a last sign that the possibility for life is finished.

Notice the parabolic character of this exchange. God said, "I am about to take the light of your eyes away from you at a stroke." What could that be? One might think "the light of your eyes" is beloved Jerusalem. In a way it is, for it is beloved Jerusalem that is being terminated. That is what the mourning is about. But more intimately and personally we are told, it is the wife of Ezekiel who is being taken away. In v. 18 his wife has died, and he is forbidden to mourn. His wife, for him so precious, is a parable for God's love of Jerusalem. As his beloved wife dies, so beloved Jerusalem must die. Ezekiel may not mourn even as God will not mourn Jerusalem. What does it mean to have silence through all of this? There must be silence because it is so *unutterable*. In chapter 24 the literature arrives at a point where nothing else can be said. The words have all been spoken. The die has been cast. Now there is only silent waiting. Now words would only trivialize. We are invited with the hopeless community to ponder the loss and leave it without speech.

The motif of prophetic silence appears one more time in 33:21–22:

> A man who had escaped from Jerusalem came to me and said, "The city has fallen."

This is the pivot in Ezekiel. The warnings have been unheeded. The righteousness God expected from Israel has been ignored. The holiness departed, because it had been intolerably mocked by Judah. The known world has caved in and none could prop it up. As the precious wife died, so the precious city ended. It could have been saved, but the saving was more costly than Judah wanted to pay. Only Judah could have made the saving possible, for God had long since left it to its own devices. Judah neither cared nor understood, and so the city had fallen.

The prophet internalized the loss. The prophet is forbidden to speak. The prophet has borne in silence even the loss of his wife and now also the beloved city. Ministry has to do with grieving silence after the warning is unheeded.

Notice that this third use of the silence is in 33:21-22, just at the very beginning of the post-587 texts of hope. The placement is crucial for the book. Because once the message of the destruction comes to Ezekiel, he says:

Now the hand of the Lord was upon me . . . and he opened my mouth . . . so my tongue was opened, and I was no longer dumb! (au. trans.)

Astonishing! The prophet is mute while the city dies. But when the city has died, when the news has come, when the loss is embraced and acknowledged, then speech is possible. It is an interesting way to think about depression. The honest, acknowledged loss does not cause immobilization. Acknowledged loss permits the return of speech and the restoration of functioning life. Ezekiel has embraced in his own life and body the failure of Judah. He has embraced it fully—drained it to the bottom of the cup. Because of this season of painful submission, the prophet is now prepared to speak with a new, positive, creative toughness. Now he speaks hope. It is a powerful hope made possible only by submission, dumbness, loss.

HOPE AT THE BREAK POINT

Ezekiel, child of the tradition, now speaks again. He speaks out of the old tradition of new possibility. In his liberated mouth, the old, old story now becomes the new, new song. He speaks in vitality, out of the tradition that had lost its vitality. The tradition has been broken. Now it is restored to power and importance. It is the tradition now passed through and transformed by the submissive loss which surprises Israel. Israel is no longer in control, but newness now becomes available. It is not a buoyant tradition but a broken tradition that now mediates new possibility through Ezekiel.

In the powerful language of chapters 34—37, 40—48,[19] Ezekiel speaks about a new future given by God beyond the lost city. The final test of vitality in ministry is to articulate concrete hope just when the community decides upon hopelessness.

In 34:1-10 Ezekiel presents a harsh analysis of the shepherds (kings) who had used their power and office in exploitative ways. By way of contrast he enunciates the new rule in which the shepherd will genuinely care for the sheep (vv. 11-16). Very likely there is editorial work here reflecting a difference of opinion in the community. On the one hand, it is Yahweh himself who is offered as the new shepherd (v. 11). On the other hand, the hope is for a new David (v. 23), but either way, the ordering of social life will be humane and just:

> I will seek the lost, and I will bring back the strayed, and I will bind up the crippled, and I will strengthen the weak, and the fat and the strong I will watch over; I will feed them in justice. (v. 16)

The newness anticipated is a restored political order with political institutions that will practice justice. The justice refused before 587 is now to be a social reality.

The most familiar new possibility is the metaphor of resurrection in 37:1-14. It is clear that the language of "dry bones" and resurrection is precisely metaphorical, for in v. 12 the promise is "I will bring you home into the land of Israel." The hope is for homecoming for exiles. It is remarkable that this prophet who spent so many words on judgment and exile is the very same one who, in a new setting, can speak about hope so powerfully and so concretely. The homecoming is not presented on the basis of political analysis. Indeed, one could not see how that could happen under the Babylonian hegemony. The point is theological, not political. It is the "wind of God" which creates a new future. That wind is beyond resistance from the empire or anyone else.

The metaphor for new possibility is shifted in chapters 43—44, which serve to counter the departure of glory in chapters 9—10. Now one can hear the flutter of the returning cherubim. The sound of fluttering wings signals the reclaiming of the temple, the return of glory, the restoration of presence, to overcome the dread of absence. But the return of the glory comes after, never before, the city is fallen. The power and rule of God are established on Sunday only after the fullness of dark Friday, never before. The hope is not spoken too soon. When it is spoken, it is overwhelming. As chapter 34 speaks of the resumption of political life, so these chapters speak about the resumption of liturgical life. Vitality in ministry depends on seeing how interrelated political and liturgical dimensions of life are.

Along with the reclaimed temple, which appeals especially to priests, 47:13—48:29 takes up a quite different metaphor and speaks about the restoration of the land of the promise. In detail the prophet delineates a new distribution of the land which is like the work of Joshua (13—19) among the peasants. The typology is poignant. Joshua 13—19 was the gift of land precisely to the ones who yearned for land and had none.[20] Now the land promise is to the exiles who must also yearn for land and have no prospect of getting any. But the promise is given. When the city falls, there is a new set of peasants, the ones waiting desperately and hopefully because they know there can be no land for them until there is a new act of redistribution.[21] When the city falls, the land can be reassigned. Only those who had too much land grieved the change because it meant the end of their monopoly (cf. Mic. 2:1-5). One may imagine that God was not one of those who had too much land. Indeed the abominations of Judah had denied God, along with the other exiles, God's safe dwelling in Jerusalem.

At the end of the speech about land redistribution, at the very end of the book, at the end of the material about hope and new possibility, a word is spoken over the city that has fallen. The fallen city is now to be the utterly restored city, indeed a new city. The name of that city, stunningly, is "Yahweh is there." What a name! What a promise! The old city had received a terrible name: "Yahweh is gone" (10:18-22). We cause the absence of God (cf. 8:6). But now a new name, a new song which speaks of city, presence, joy all given by the faithful power of God, just at the "null point."[22] Passionate ministry is to be able to stand in that "null point" and to speak a new world and a new city against the despair of the exile.

This Ezekiel, who had submitted to his limited role of watchman and who had submitted to the silence imposed by God, has his toughest say in 36:22–32. The premise of everything has now changed. We have seen that in chapter 18, Ezekiel has appealed for serious righteousness and a redirected loyalty. Such serious faith, however, did not emerge in Judah. Finally, Ezekiel came to realize that the evil was so massive as to be hopeless. If there had been a turn, the city might have been saved, but it was not to be. There could be no turn. The city could not be saved.

However, after failing, after the city has fallen and speech is given back, Ezekiel speaks a new word on this issue. Now he does not seek repentance. He knows that is impossible. Instead he speaks words of radical grace from the side of God. The new righteousness and the new heart of which Judah is incapable are now to be given as free gifts.

> A new heart I will give you, and a new spirit I will put within you; and I will take out of your flesh the heart of stone and give you a heart of flesh.
>
> (36:26)

These replace the old hard heart and the old failed breath. God will do for God's people what they could not do for themselves. This is the good news of free gift.

This word of grace does not mean that Ezekiel has caved in. He has not become soft or romantic. He is, in his new hopeful message, still tough. This is not sniveling graciousness, but it is the glory of God turned toward this people. The glory gives life, but in a tough way:

> It is not for your sake that I will act, says the Lord God. Let that be known to you (v. 22) . . . . but for the sake of my holy name. (v. 32)

Israel is the lucky benefactor, but the new age and the new city and the new possibility are rooted only in the indicative of God's holiness. God will not be useful to Israel even at the end. God will only care for God. In this regard Ezekiel is very different from Jeremiah. Jeremiah could speak of God's love for Israel (31:3), but Ezekiel does not. Here there is only holiness and the zeal of God to protect the holy name, but that has unspeakable results for Israel. The crumbs that fall from the table of God's holiness are enough to sustain a people in holiness, even if it is unintentional.

4

"FOR THE SAKE OF MY HOLY NAME"

(EZEKIEL 36:22-32)

Ezekiel, like jeremiah, watched while the city was destroyed. He traveled the same road as Jeremiah. He also had to speak the truth. He had to offer pastoral care among exiles. But he saw through a different lens, and so made a different discernment. Whereas Jeremiah speaks with passion and pathos, Ezekiel hints about little of either. He is much more cold, reflective, and symmetrical in his perception. Jeremiah in both grief and newness is a voice of unreason. But Ezekiel is almost syllogistic in his reasoning, building the case tightly, step by step, until the conclusion is unavoidable.

Ezekiel has also seen the coming death of all that was precious. Chapters 1—24 build the case that this must happen. He shows why it must happen. The literature builds to a dramatic moment when in 33:21 the messenger comes finally to say, "The city has fallen." The literature is shaped so that we have come to expect and wait for the word.[1] It is almost like the relaxation of dramatic tension. We had waited for so long in dread and in silence. We had known the destruction was unavoidable, but it had not happened. And until the city fell, one was never sure. "The city has fallen." Chapters 1—24 tell why. The language overlaps with Jeremiah, but the focus is much more God-centered for Ezekiel. Judah did not let God be God. Judah failed to reckon with the awful jealousy of God who will be taken seriously (5:13). Judah had grown accustomed to God, so at ease that God was taken for granted. Judah had long since forgotten that there is a zone of danger around this terrible God, almost a substantive power which the priests sort out into "clean and unclean."

The political language of rebellion is found in Ezekiel (cf. 2:3, 6-8), but the preferred language of Ezekiel which intends to elevate the majesty of God is not *political* or even *covenantal* language but *ritual* language of purity and contamination. This is not moral or sexual purity but ritual qualification. Because of ritual failure, the exiles are sent to eat their bread in uncleanness (4:13). Judah is indicted for having defiled the sanctuary, rendering it ritually off limits (5:11). The altars and incense altars have been abandoned (6:4), the ornaments of worship are so misused that all of it is made unclean. This language is strange to us, because we live such horizontal lives in which everything is reduced to morality.

But this awesome ritual language is more basic than the language of covenant or of politics.[2] It asks, Under what circumstances can the holy God be present? This is the language of *presence*.[3] Jerusalem is precious because it is where God is present. But in 8:6, Ezekiel has God make this unprecedented statement: "They are doing a great abomination to drive me from my sanctuary." The defilement causes God's removal, because God will not stay in such environs which have the smell of death. Where God is banished, there is a departure of God's glory, an absence of God's transcendent purpose, of God's protective attention, the failure of the power for life. The gift of life is available only where God's transcendent power is present. Now it is gone, banished in the face of defilement, and where banished, there can only be death.

Ezekiel will not have God so dishonored, as though God did not matter. Even the acts of God's *judgment* are understood as a show of God's *sovereignty*. In 6:10 when Judah suffers, "they shall know I am Yahweh."[4] When the slain fall, "they shall know I am Yahweh" (6:7). When the land is desolate, "they shall know I am Yahweh" (6:14). One might wonder what good it does to know Yahweh, if it is all deathly. But that issue is not one for Ezekiel. Yahweh is not a means but an end. Everything flows from this recognition. Yahweh is known through negative power, known as the one who can be absent, as the one whose glory can depart, whose life-giving power can be withdrawn. We consider this text (36:22–32) because in broad outline I mean to suggest that is our situation in life. The life-giving power of God seems not to be given in the conventional forms on which we have presumed and relied. Much of our life is in jeopardy. We are genuinely at a loss. In some crucial ways, we are the generation for whom the city has fallen. We are left to ponder: What now? Is there something after the city has fallen? Or shall we imagine that for us, unlike Ezekiel, the defiled city is immune and will not finally fall?

THE HOLINESS OF GOD

Ezekiel's portrayal of Jerusalem is a tale of God's holiness. The question I raise is how holiness is a ground for hope. We should not rush to hope, however. Ezekiel is not preoccupied with hope but with holiness. Perhaps hope will follow when holiness is rightly discerned.

The holiness of God, as Ezekiel understands it, may be considered in two dimensions and then in two stages. The two dimensions of holiness are important to distinguish. First, it is possible, and attractive to us, to take God's holiness as a cognate of righteousness, that is, as a category of ethical concern. This is not remote from Ezekiel, as in chapter 18.[5] God's holiness requires obedience to the commandments. Where there is disobedience, there will surely be punishment. But if the holiness of God is experienced only in disobedience, it is not a force for hope. Then holiness only permits the newness that is wrought by obedience, and the obedience available in Judah is not an adequate obedience. It is important that God's holiness yield hope not measured by Judah's obedience.

More elementally, holiness is not an ethical but a theological category. It concerns not God's will but God's person. Or, if one may put it so, it concerns God's Godness. Under this rubric one is more likely to speak about God's unutterableness, God's massiveness, rather than God's fidelity. We are so preoccupied with God's relatedness, God being for us, that we do not attend enough to God's hiddenness,[6] God's weighty concern for God's self, God's own way in heaven and on earth. As *pathos* is Jeremiah's critical insight into God, it is *holiness* which marks the God of Ezekiel. That, of course, is why Ezekiel is less congenial to us, because this God attends only to God's own way in creation and is not noticeably for us. We must take care not to reduce and translate God's holiness solely into moral categories, because that draws God too closely into the orbit of good and evil, which in the first instance does not really touch God.

In our use of holiness, then, I shall mean not only righteous will but also unutterable splendor. The first dimension causes God to attend closely to Jerusalem, the second gives God amazing freedom from Jerusalem and from everything else. In light of that distinction, we may observe Ezekiel's two-stage theology. It is not unlike that of Jeremiah, but it is done with much more discipline. The first step in this magisterial theology is the *work of judgment* which is extensively articulated in chapters 1—24. It is God's holiness that finds the corruption, disobedience, uncleanness intolerable. This holiness has to do with cultic presence. But this holiness cannot and will not be present amidst ritual defilement, which renders worship impossible and places all of life in jeopardy. God's holiness is intolerant of the corruption that leads to the end of the city, the ritual arrangement, and the political process. That is the first stage of God's holiness, an inability to compromise with worship or life that is incongruous with God's own holy person. In such contexts, judgment must come.

The second dimension of holiness for Ezekiel's God is the *work of hope*. After the judgment, when the city has fallen, does it follow that God's holiness has finished its work and now withdrawn from the field with nothing left to do? Is God's holiness only interested in and capable of crushing the unacceptable? God's judging action is enough to let the nations know "I am Yahweh." But it is evident in Ezekiel 33—37 and 40—48 that the holiness of God is also a constructive force making new life possible. My argument, which I believe is faithful to Ezekiel, is that real newness is possible only out of God's holiness, which is given in raw power after the judgment. The newness after judgment results from the second act of God's holiness. The newness made possible by holiness is a whole new world of power and mercy, a reorganization of public life. But this reorganization of public life is not possible if life is reduced to human control. It is precisely this indefatigable power of God's holiness that makes newness possible. My urging, then, is that the holiness of God is a theological theme we do well to recover if there is a will among us for newness. Without this focus on the holiness of God, we are consigned to life as a profaned, flat human enterprise that can only end in despair.

GOD AS GROUND FOR HOPE

Ezekiel 36:22–32 is an odd and strikingly powerful text, one I have rediscovered for myself only recently. I believe it is peculiarly urgent for our theological situation. Attend to it and notice where your imagination is led:

> Therefore say to the house of Israel, Thus says the Lord God: "It is not for your sake, O house of Israel, that I am about to act, but for the sake of my holy name, which you have profaned among the nations to which you came. And I will vindicate the holiness of my great name, which has been profaned among the nations, and which you have profaned among them; and the nations will know that I am the Lord, says the Lord God, when through you I vindicate my holiness before their eyes. For I will take you from the nations, and gather you from all the countries, and bring you into your own land. I will sprinkle clean water upon you, and you shall be clean from all your uncleannesses, and from all your idols I will cleanse you. A new heart I will give you, and a new spirit I will put within you; and I will take out of your flesh the heart of stone and give you a heart of flesh. And I will put my spirit within you and cause you to walk in my statutes and be careful to observe my ordinances. You shall dwell in the land which I gave to your fathers; and you shall be my people, and I will be your God. And I will deliver you from all your uncleannesses; and I will summon the grain and make it abundant and lay no famine upon you. I will make the fruit of the tree and the increase of the field abundant, that you may never again suffer the disgrace of famine among the nations. Then you will remember your evil ways and your deeds that were not good; and you will loathe yourselves for your iniquities and your abominable deeds. It is not for your sake that I will act, says the Lord God; let that be known to you. Be ashamed and confounded for your ways, O house of Israel. (36:22–32)

The text is found in the second half of the Book of Ezekiel, in which the prophet offers visions and interpretations of the newness God will work out of the ruins of the fallen city.[7] This text is placed in an immediate context of marvelous hope. In chapter 34 we are given a harsh judgment of foolish shepherds (rulers) who are self-serving, who exploit the sheep only for themselves. All these shepherds are under judgment and are contrasted with Yahweh who will himself be the real shepherd in time to come, the good shepherd who seeks out lost, exiled sheep:

> I, I myself will search for my sheep and will seek them out . . . . I will seek out my sheep, and I will rescue them from all places where they have been scattered . . . and I will bring them out from the peoples. I will gather them from the countries. I will bring them into their own land. I will feed them . . . I will feed them with good pasture . . . I myself will be the shepherd of my sheep and I will make them lie down . . . I will seek the lost . . . I will bring back the strayed. I will strengthen the weak and the fat and the strong I will watch over. I will feed them in justice. (34:11–16; au. trans.)

Chapter 34 offers a most eloquent statement about God's powerful intervention. The text exploits the metaphor of shepherd in such a way that even Psalm 23 looks thin beside it. The text is in fact talking about the end of exile. What is most remarkable is that, except for the reference to a new David in vv. 23–24, it is Yahweh alone who presides over the new community. There is no human agent or mediator. God's own person is engaged in the historical process, looking toward a homecoming.

This assertion comes right before the chapter with which we are concerned.[8] Afterward (26:22–32) comes Ezekiel's most familiar vision, the valley of the dry bones (37:1–14). That, of course, is a powerful use of the metaphor of resurrection, wrought by God's spirit which gives new life. It is clear from v. 12 that the resurrection metaphor is about homecoming and restoration for exiles. In 37:15–23 follows the ecumenical vision of north and south reunited.

The question posed by these marvelous promises is: On what basis? Why will God do this? How can we know to trust such incredible promises? Two bases can be immediately dismissed as offering no hope. First, there is no hope in Israel's repentance or change of heart. Ezekiel has appealed for that (chapter 18), but it would not happen. Finally the prophet gives up on that possibility.[9] But the ground for hope established in Jeremiah is also not operative here. Jeremiah has grounded hope finally in God's yearning pathos, in something like mother love which is so passionate that God cannot finally resist the deep power of God's own passionate desire. There is nothing like that in Ezekiel. This holy God evidences no such inclination, no jealousy for Israel which would cause such a move of passion. Then what is the ground for this staggering hope? Chapter 36 suggests that Ezekiel, stern theologian that he is, offers a tougher, more basic ground of hope.

The passage forms an envelope of three basic themes structured in three concentric circles:

1. At the center (36:24–30) is an extensive series of first-person assertions on the part of God. They announce what God will do. The rhetoric is important. The situation of judgment leaves no other resource available to the community. Nothing now remains except for God to speak a new, unfettered word. Thus God promises:

I will take you from the nations
I will gather you
I will bring you to your land
I will sprinkle clean water
I will cleanse you.

This first series is an announcement of homecoming. Since the exile was caused by ritual pollution, now ritual cleansing is offered. Israel is made acceptable to live again in God's presence by this act of washing.

The series continues with the word order inverted for purposes of emphasis:

A new heart I will give you
A new spirit I will put
I will take out the heart of stone and give a heart of flesh
I will put my spirit within you.

The first series is *geographical*: homecoming. This second series of first person assertion is *covenantal*. An organ transplant is required for this hard-hearted people to be in covenant. The prophets had asked for a changed heart (see Deut. 30:6; Jer. 4:4), but Israel is incapable of change (see Jer. 13:23). The new heart and new mind will permit obedience (Ezek. 36:27). New life given by God is not a life of self-indulgence, but is a life in which obedience is possible. This part of the passage culminates in v. 28 with the promise of land, and then the formal symmetrical statement of covenant:

You will be my people, I will be your God.

The relation is restored. Israel not only comes home to the land but comes back to the community of its identity. This is an act of incredible graciousness, given what Israel had done.

The third series following *homecoming* and *new covenant* is *new creation*:

> I will summon the grain and make it abundant and lay no famine on you.
> I will make the fruit of the tree and the increase of the field abundant, that you may never again suffer the disgrace of famine among the nations. (36:29-30)

The abundance of creation is mobilized so that Israel need be no suppliant for food.[10] Creation is mobilized because Yahweh is sovereign and creation is obedient. This is indeed a starting over in every aspect of life.

2. The assertion of God's new deeds stands at the center of this text. Framing it on both sides (in 36:22-23 and v. 31), the evil and disobedience are stated one more time. In 36:22-23 the disobedience is profaning the name of God. The verb is *halal* which means "to put to common use," and therefore to cheapen, trivialize, and nullify the holiness of the name. This word pair, *profane/holy* is not quite equivalent to *clean/unclean* but it approximates it (see 22:26; 44:23). The final outcome of Israel's rebellion is that God's Godness is mocked, God's sovereignty is diminished. In v. 31 the corresponding indictment concerns "iniquities and evil deeds." Presumably these statements are given to dismiss decisively any notion that Israel has anything to contribute to the newness. Israel is completely disqualified and is a powerless suppliant who can only receive what will be given. We have, at the center of the passage, a summary of God's new intention and a denial that Israel has any contribution to the new possibility.

3. It is, however, the third and outer ring of the passage that interests us the most:

> It is not for your sake, O House of Israel, that I am about to act, but for the sake of my holy name which you have profaned among the nations to which you came. . . .
> I will vindicate the holiness of my great name . . . and the nations will know that I am Yahweh, says the Lord God, when through you I vindicate my holiness before your eyes. (36:22-23; au. trans.)

> It is not for your sake that I will act, says the Lord God; let that be known to you. Be ashamed and confounded for your ways, O house of Israel. (v. 36:32)

I regard this as one of the most dangerous and stunning texts in the Bible, for it sets God's free, unfettered sovereignty at a distance from Israel. All our conventional, relational, covenantal categories of love and mercy, justice and faithfulness, are here set aside. God's pathos, as evidenced in Jeremiah, is important. But it has its limits. What happens after God's caring compassion is exhausted? What then? Ezekiel's judgment is that Israel's abominable behavior has pushed God's caring commitment to the extreme and beyond it. What happens when we exhaust God's mother love?

This text would answer: Then there is God, in all of God's prickly, unaccommodating self-concern. God's name, God's good name, God's reputation are important to God. God does not want to be taken lightly, not by Israel, and not by the surrounding nations who watched. The nations have watched closely. It is like people in a restaurant watching a family with small children.[11] The children are tired and do not act well. The parents are nervous and react. They are also tired and do not do well either. Not much is at stake for the children because they are just children. But the parents know their reputation is at stake in this encounter. How adequate they want to be, how composed and caring, how able to cope. They feel and act as though their entire reputation as caring, adequate adults is at stake in this issue. The profaning of the name of the parents means that a reputation gets around town that they cannot manage.

That is what has happened to Yahweh, the God of Israel. The whole history of Israel until 587 had been one long tantrum by Israel. Israel never obeyed, according to Ezekiel, not even from the very beginning. Israel was always challenging, profaning, trivializing, mocking, exploiting. God's long-suffering love took a lot of it and endured. The nations, meanwhile, watched. They watched carefully and Yahweh knew they were watching. Yahweh finally became embarrassed, ashamed, and humiliated. The violation of Yahweh's honor and good reputation is a serious matter. Finally it is so serious that Yahweh will tolerate no more. It is this profaning of the name that leads to the destruction of Jerusalem. Yahweh will be pushed only so far. Yahweh has now been pushed that far, and so the end has been wrought (7:2; see Amos 8:2).

Unlike Jeremiah, Ezekiel gives few clues to the internal life of God. Perhaps Ezekiel does not know. More likely he finds it neither interesting nor important. What Ezekiel finds interesting and important is God's public life among the nations. The massive destruction was accomplished. It was done because Yahweh would not tolerate any longer the deep disrespect of Israel. But as such destruction often does, it did not gain respect for Yahweh among the gods and the nations. Like lashing out at a child in the restaurant, it may seem necessary and it might even feel good, but it seldom wins the response of those who stand and watch. So Yahweh found that in order to regain honor, to reassert holiness of the name, one more thing is necessary, a show of positive power. The negative show of power in destruction had failed to convince.

In the third layer of this text, the outside circle at beginning and end, there is this: *not for your sake, for me, for my sake*. The RSV has, "I will vindicate the holiness of my great name." The verb is in the *pi'el*. I will make holy my name, I will make holy what you profane. What you have treated as common, I will make freely, majestically special. I will do it for my own sake. The only way God can do such a positive act to enhance God's own honor is to act positively toward Israel. Yahweh has no other arena in which to show the nations his positive sovereignty.

Thus the verbs in these verses concerning Yahweh's activity are all positive and all serve Israel:

I will take you
I will gather
I will bring you
I will sprinkle clean water
I will give a new heart
I will put a new spirit
I will take out the heart of stone
I will give a heart of flesh
I will put my spirit in you
I will deliver you
I will summon grain
I will make increase

"I, I, I, I, I, I—for you, for you, for you." But it is no longer because I care, because I love you, because I hurt, because I yearn. All of that is spent and forfeited. No appeal to covenant love, pathos, or fidelity is made. Now it is only God. Then nations will watch, and will draw the conclusion that will restore God's good name and reputation.

The holiness of God serves only God. It has no other purpose, no partner to take into account. It enters no other service. It cannot be harnessed or presumed upon. For Ezekiel, God is not one who gives God's self away. God keeps God's reputation very close, treasures it, nurtures it, enhances it.

But how odd. This God finally is inalienably related to Israel and has no life apart from this people. This God will not be enhanced, except by acts toward Israel. God must do good even for the one in whom God has no positive interest. Such statements about God may sound hard-nosed and calloused. This theological posture does not resonate very easily with our therapeutic inclination, not as well as Jeremiah's suffering God, but, I submit, we arrive here at a surer ground of hope. Indeed, this harsh claim is the bedrock base for serious evangelical faith. It asserts that all hope for the future rests in the very character of God, for this God will take seriously being God.

Ezekiel 36:22–32 is thus set in three concentric circles. At the center is *the new possibility for Israel* to be God's partner (vv. 24–30). At the intermediate stage, only of subordinate interest, is *the disqualification of Israel* because of sin. Israel produces nothing useful for the future with God (vv. 23, 31). At the outside of the text is the massive *reality of God's self-concern* (vv. 22–23a, 32). The theological interest of this text is that the inner circle concerns *a hope for Israel* (new heart and new life). At the outer circle is *the power of God's holiness.* The issue is how the combative statement and the core of new possibility relate to each other, how God's holiness and Israel's hope touch each other.

Ezekiel has a profound sense of Israel's sin. He argues and asserts this sense for twenty-four chapters. No ground for hope is to be found in Israel. If there is then to be hope, it must be found in God. It is God's free, unfettered, massive holiness which has as a by-product hope for Israel. Chapters 34—37, 40—48 are about just such a reconstruction for Israel out of the "null point."[12] In the zero hour, Israel has run out of options.[13] Its despair is powered by its guilt. There is nothing left, no impetus, no motivation, no energy, no possibility. In the face of this, we have fourteen chapters of possibility. None of this possibility for the future is owed to Israel. Possibility is given to Israel because God has no alternative way to clear God's honorable name. This strange theology is a rich pastoral resource in any situation where guilt produces despair. The deep guilt in this nuclear neighborhood of ours drives us to despair. We are left to ask if in the very character of God there is ground for hope in spite of what we know about ourselves. God's free holiness does not make God indifferent, as we might expect. Instead, God's free holiness presses God to act for the sake of one who evokes no love on God's part. This is good news for extreme situations of failure and profanation!

"IT IS NOT FOR YOUR SAKE."

Ezekiel 36:22–32 needs to be heard in context. To whom is this text addressed—and why? Who needed to hear it? We know little about the specifics of Ezekiel's contemporaries, so we must discern what we can from the text. Who does this text mean to refute?

As we have seen, this text occurs midst the promissory passages of 34—37. (Chapter 35 is not much help because it is about Mount Seir and Edom and does not address Judah.) But chapters 34 and 37 are texts that concern the reconstruction of the community after the exile. Specifically 34:22–23 alludes to an active Davidic hope, which we also know from Haggai and Zechariah.[14]

But why in our text does the promise, both at the beginning and the end, assert that, "It is not for your sake"? I propose that this text intends to combat the opinion prevalent in exilic Judaism that assumes the restoration is based on the merit of the recovering community. Or more subtly, the assumption that God has made a commitment that God now must honor. Or to press the point further, the text means to refute the idea that somehow God is committed to and enmeshed in a social system or a political arrangement and that God's action is limited to or controlled by the needs or possibilities of a particular historical setting. The text combats the notion that God has an intrinsic organismic linkage to this or any social arrangement.

This text refutes the temptation of exilic Judah to understand God in terms of God's usefulness, the capacity to harness God to certain social objectives.[15] Such a temptation is never done blatantly or directly, but the end result is that God is included in a functional view of reality, in which God functions instrumentally for other purposes.[16] That is, God is then not an end but a means toward another end, namely the establishment of a particular historical arrangement. The text resists the idea that somehow God's freedom is circumscribed by this historical process and is useful in its establishment. The freedom of God's sovereignty here asserted serves to relativize and jeopardize every historical effort to program God for Judah's purposes. Observe how odd that must have sounded. Alternative opinion must have held that there is hope because God is irrevocably committed to the temple priesthood or to the dynasty or to some such historical form. Hope based in temple and dynasty reduces God to patron rather that sovereign. Ezekiel makes the more difficult case that hope depends precisely on the opposite. Hope depends on God *not* having such a commitment, because new possibility depends on God not being so confined or restricted or committed.

One can see how the issue of God's freedom is joined in a very serious argument. If God is unalterably committed to a historical arrangement—the free market system, democratic socialism, classless society—we might manage the future. Conversely, if God be free, God may work a surprise. This latter freedom requires not predictability but profound trust. Which of these offers a surer hope? It depends on whether God is to be trusted or whether only a particular social outcome is to be trusted. To rely on a certain social outcome, however, is not trust but only ideology. If one's hope is reduced to only a certain outcome, God is not trusted. God is *used* but not trusted. I propose then, that this text requires exilic Judaism to clarify its hope, to find out if hope is really in the holiness of God or if one's hope is limited to a particular social outcome (see the same issue in Job 1:9). The latter way claims to know too much about the intent of God and reduces the ways of God to our preferred ways.

A PARABLE OF SUBMISSION AND SELF-SUFFICIENCY

The choice presented by Ezek. 36:22–32 is to harness God to our preferred schemes (which is a form of co-opted hope) or to hope in trust for whatever God chooses to give. I suggest that the choice presented by Ezekiel is extended and illuminated by the parable of Jesus in Luke 18:9–14.[17]

The parable of the Pharisee and the publican draws the contrast sharply and unmistakably between the two parties who pray. The parable is told to "some who trusted in themselves, that were righteous and despised others" (v. 9). The parable is aimed at those who imagine that the ground for security and well-being and finally salvation is located within themselves.

The first man who went up to the temple to pray is a Pharisee, a good religious liberal. He embodies in the story the ones who trusted in themselves. The story is told so that the Pharisee is only once removed from the listener, so that the listener should not have great difficulty participating in the story and finding his or her proper role. The Pharisee is the religiously confident person, or we may say, in secularized form, the psychologically assured, the politically bold, the economically buoyant. These descriptions are all variations on the theme that the justification for my existence is found in me. (Note that the term "justification" works nicely in two ways, both for the theological issue of justification and for the kind of social vindication sought by the widow in the preceding parable.) Justification for my existence could be more casually rendered: What is my excuse for living? This Pharisee is able to say, which the story seems to support, "I am my excuse for living." "I am not like the others, extortioners, unjust, adulterers. I fast twice a week. I give a tithe of all I get." Notice all the "I" statements. The source and initiative for his self-understanding are reflected in the grammatical structure of his statements.

In the life of such a person, such a church, such a nation, prayer becomes a self-announcement: "to whom it may concern." The prayer is cast as thanks, but the rhetoric does not grant God much credit. (See the prayer of David: 2 Sam. 7:18–29.)[18] In such a life, such a self-understanding, such a self-presentation, where is there room left for God? To be sure, in Luke 18:11, the prayer is addressed to God. But who is this God? I suggest the God of this man and this prayer is a partner in virtue, an element in the system, a symbol for religious self-justification. God has become a usable and useful object. The purpose of God is to deliver the agreed-upon benefits of the system. But notice this system of life management neither wants nor needs nor allows any free initiative from God. God is useful precisely as God cooperates in keeping the self-system functioning. Such a "useful" God allows no place for the free, abrasive holiness of God known in Ezekiel. When the holiness of God is acknowledged, the whole system of virtue and security may be nullified.

Consider how this Pharisee in the parable might receive the announcements of God at the beginning and end of our passage in Ezek. 36:22-23, 32:

> It is not for your sake . . . but for the sake of my holy name. . . . I will vindicate the holiness of my great name. . . . It is not for your sake that I will act. . . .

Israel is in exile. Israel has been destroyed. Israel has been given the grounds for the judgment of God. Now newness begins to happen. A new shepherd is announced. A new spirit is among the dry bones. A new covenant of peace, a coming out of exile. An experience of new possibility is offered.

Israel dared to hope. But Israel also began to discuss how God's future could be and on what basis God's promises could come to fruition. It is not enough to receive a fresh gift of a new heart. Some in Israel began to imagine that the newness happens because God has found something valuable in Israel, or simply because of God's great love for Israel, or because God has a deep commitment to Israel, to override the system and make it work one more time. Israel engages in *a misunderstanding of self*, imagining that it is more valued by God than it is. Israel engages in *a misunderstanding of God*, imagining that God is more enmeshed with and beholden than in fact God is. Israel in fact engages in narcissism, imagining that God exists for the sake of Israel (cf. Rom. 12:3).

There is an interesting parallel between the parable of the Pharisee and the publican and the decree of Ezekiel. The man in the parable says, in his pride, anxiety, narcissism "as he prayed thus to himself":

> I thank thee that I am the way I am—and not like the others. (Luke 18:11; au. trans.)

As you know, the Pharisee in the parable was not vindicated. It is the holy God who is vindicated, who is in no way shaped by or in need of this virtuous prayer. To this practitioner of utilitarianism religion, the God of Ezekiel says, "not for your sake will I act, but for the sake of my holiness."

The other man in the parable, the tax collector, is not so interesting to us, perhaps because we do not identify so readily with him. The parable intends it that way. The terseness of the picture and the economy of words in v. 13 matches the sparseness of his person. Both the style and the person stand in contrast to the first man. The narrator has mockingly used many extra words to portray this Pharisee of many parts who will have no share in the kingdom.

Now the second man prays. Even in the parable he had to wait to pray, because he is never first, always second—or even last. The tax collector, embodiment of genuine self-abasement, speaks in a low tone. He will not lift his eyes or his voice, because he knows the incredible gap between himself and the one to whom he prays. For the first man, there was no gap. It was an easy conversation, bridged by many words about self. The speech of this second man does not try to bridge the gap, because there is nothing about his words or his person which could make a bridge. His style, his speech do not try to compete with God's Godness, do not crowd God, because he has nothing with which to crowd God. He yields himself and throws himself toward the throne with no self-regard.

The parable hinges on one word of the tax collector: mercy. "Have mercy on me" (Luke 18:13). The tax collector asked for that for which the Pharisee never asked. He understands, as the Pharisee does not, that God's freedom, not God's domestication, is the ground for possibility. There is mercy for this man, and that mercy can only be rooted in God's holiness. Mercy that is owed or coerced or previously committed is not mercy. It is only mercy when it is given freely and when it is received as freely given.

This second man alone in the parable is justified and vindicated. It is this man to whom the promises of Ezekiel 36:24–28 are granted:

I will take you
I will gather you
I will sprinkle clean water

I will give you a new heart
I will take away your heart of flesh
I will put my spirit within you
You will dwell in the land of your fathers
You shall be mine, I will be your God.

To this man, Ezekiel's God hardly needed to say, "not for your sake." This man knew deep in his bones that God was holy and unapproachable. It never occurred to him that God might be useful. He had no designs on God, no use to which to put God, and therefore no presumption on God.

The parable ends tersely with its inescapable verdict:

One was justified and one was not.
Everyone who exalts himself will be humbled,
but who humbles himself will be exalted. (Luke 18:14; au. trans.)

ON THE WAY BACK HOME?

It remains to make a connection between this massive word from Ezekiel and our situation of faith. This harsh word from Ezekiel is a part of the Bible that may be oddly pertinent to our situation. In our time Ludwig Feuerbach is difficult to refute. He argued that faith in God is a projection of our best hopes and our best selves, that God has no real independent existence, but that God talk is projection and therefore idolatry. All the contemporary heirs of Friedrich Schleiermacher[19] run dangerously close to the same affirmation and practice, and then seek to make a virtue out of it. Ezekiel 36:22–32 affirms that *the reality of God's holiness* must be a theological question among us, with particular reference to the subjective consciousness of our theological climate. Such a theological affirmation on the face of it is something of an affront to our situation, for it appears as intellectually primitive. It is not Ezekiel's particular primitive articulation that troubles us, but his raw claim of unfettered sovereignty that is so problematic.

1. Ours is essentially a *narcissistic culture*. The pathology of narcissism is enormously supported by consumer advertising, for that enterprise rests on a value system of satiation and self-indulgence. Moreover, it is supported by much psychology that has rootage in voices

like Abraham Maslow but has been carried to demonic ends in popularization.[20] These psychologies may have been important in opening up alternatives to rigid and authoritarian modes, but they themselves have now become destructively authoritarian.

Every one of us knows how easily the life of the church is caught in this narcissism in which appeal to the gospel is grounded in what it will do for us in terms of intimacy, problem solving, marriage saving, and so forth. None of these are in themselves wrong, but when they become the end, goal, and ground of appeal, it becomes pathological, because it is not "for the sake of my holy name."

2. For those who are not excessively caught in personal narcissism, we are more likely to be committed to *social utilitarianism*. We understand God in terms of God's will, what God wants done, and how we shall be about the business of doing it. The loss in our rhetoric and in theology of God's free sovereignty is matched by our penchant to link God to life systems. This can be done in intellectually sophisticated ways, as for example in some forms of process theology which want somehow to present God as embedded in the life process.

3. For most of us utilitarianism (i.e., God's usefulness) is in fact *ideological*. God is drawn into and identified with a variety of social commitments which we advocate. It is so easy then for conservatives to identify with God, because they know so fully the mind of God, to present God as a partisan in the struggle against homosexuality, or in a crusade against communism, even in justification of the arms race. Liberals also know the mind of God and know God is pro-busing and pro-choice and all of the other themes of justice to which one is committed.[21]

Drawing too close to God's will can, of course, be much more benign. It can be simply that prayer is good because it keeps families together, and tithing is good because one feels better, and worship is good because one gets refueled, and singing in the choir is good because one meets nice people. All of which is true but does not touch the reality of God.

All such subjective, narcissistic, utilitarian, ideological postures finally become burdensome, because they require us to know too much and claim too much and do too much. On most days it will work, but not for Ezekiel. And, I think, also not for us just now.

It is staggering and reprimanding and liberating to hear said, "Not for your sake, but for the sake of my name." All our feverish self-justification is set in perspective. We need not claim for ourselves so much in prayer because finally prayer is an act of yielding, as the needful man in the Lukan parable knows. Newness, one learns as one moves from Ezekiel 36 to the dry bones of 37, is not merely another church priority. In this society paralyzed by nuclear fear, shamed by battered women and children, beset with survival issues, newness is wrought out of God's holiness. Newness comes only from God, who will give it in God's own freedom. That may be psychologically ambiguous and sociologically problematic, but theologically and pastorally the claim is clear and hope-filled. Our lives are set back in perspective. For the times when we cannot say with Jeremiah, "It is because I yearn for you," we may hear with Ezekiel, "not for your sake, but for mine." The load is lifted. We begin again. The bones rattle. The air stirs. We could be on our way back home to our true community.

PART 3

ONLY MEMORY ALLOWS
POSSIBILITY

5

SECOND ISAIAH— HOMECOMING TO A NEW HOME

WE ARE MORE LIKELY to be attracted to 2 Isaiah than to Jeremiah, certainly more drawn to it than to Ezekiel. It is buoyant literature of hope exquisitely expressed. "Second Isaiah" refers to Isaiah 40—55, a literature set deep in the Babylonian exile, commonly dated to 540 B.C.E., just as the Babylonian empire was about to collapse in the face of rising Persian power.

Powerful as it is, the literature of 2 Isaiah cannot be understood and cannot be used without linkage to Jeremiah and to Ezekiel. Second Isaiah, as Handel has made so powerfully clear, is marvelously filled with promises. But those promises are addressed only to people in exile who have seen the city fall (40:2) and have suffered the loss of their entire world of faith. The power of the hope found in this poetry is not likely to be felt without the conflict of Jeremiah and without the toughness of Ezekiel. The promises are not available to us or effective for us while we are people who cling to the old city and to old organizations of reality. To use the poetry of homecoming without the prior literature of *exile* is an offer of cheap grace. It is important that the "new thing" of 2 Isaiah comes after a long season of exilic discontent. That discontent, failure, and grief are evidenced either in the poet quoting what must have been said (or thought) by exiles, or in the refutation of their complaints from which we may deduce the expression of doubt and grief:

> Why do you say, O Jacob,
>   and speak, O Israel,

"My way is hid from the Lord,
  and my right is disregarded by my God"? (Isa. 40:27)

But Zion said, "The Lord has forgotten me." (49:14; au. trans.)

Is my hand shortened, that it cannot redeem?
  Or have I no power to deliver? (50:2)

On the basis of literary genre, historical allusions, and theological formulations, the literature of Isaiah 40—55 has been judged to be distinct from Isaiah 1—39 (1 Isaiah). Its context is apparently the Babylonian exile of the sixth century B.C.E. The poetry of these chapters is concerned with the end of the Babylonian empire (cf. Isaiah 46—47) and the rise of Persia under Cyrus (cf. 44:28; 45:1). Cyrus practiced a benevolent imperial policy that permitted deported groups to return to their homeland. As Jeremiah saw Babylon under Nebuchadnezzar as an agent of Yahweh's judgment, so 2 Isaiah sees Persia under Cyrus as an agent of Yahweh's restorative action. The idea of being rescued by a Gentile must have been radical enough to evoke serious resistance (see 45:9-13 in response to such resistance).

More recently scholars have begun to question the notion that Isaiah 40—55 is a literature that can be treated apart from Isaiah 1—39.[1] It has been noticed afresh that chapters 40—55 have important and intentional connections to chapters 1—39 and that this relationship in the Book of Isaiah is more than an accidental juxtaposition. Rather, it is suggested, the "new thing" of God's deliverance (cf. Isa. 43:18-19) is intended precisely as a countertheme to God's judgment in chapters 1—39. These two scholarly positions, critical and canonical, are now in tension among scholars, with no resolution in sight. Our particular treatment of Isaiah 40—55 here can be sustained in either scholarly judgment, because we appeal to the imaginative practice of the poetry and not to historical facticity. Our exposition posits a theological situation of exile and newness, without respect to specific historical location.

THREE METAPHORS FOR "REREADING" ISRAEL'S LIFE

The poetry of 2 Isaiah is shaped by powerful poetic metaphors.
  The social, historical setting for this poetry is exile. The poet thus

must be heard through the metaphor of *exile*. The words grow out of and are aimed at an alienated community (cf. Psalm 137). The central fact of the community of 2 Isaiah was the power and authority of Babylonian definitions of reality (cf. Isa. 39:1-8). Babylonian cultural voices in many ways shaped Jews just as they succeeded in shaping everything and everyone else in the empire. In as many ways as possible, it was the ideological intent of the empire to talk Jews out of Jewish perceptions of reality and into Babylonian definitions of reality, to define life in terms of Babylonian values, Babylonian hopes, and Babylonian fears. Jeremiah (25:9; 27:6) had judged Babylonian triumph to be the will of Yahweh, but in the new circumstance and new generation of 2 Isaiah, it is now Yahweh's will to have Israel depart from the alien empire (Isa. 52:11-12). God will gather the displaced (43:5), releasing them from Babylon (43:14). Yahweh will send Cyrus to accomplish the release of this displaced community (45:1-4), in order that Israel may come home with joy to make a new beginning in restored Jerusalem (54:12-14).

The metaphor of Babylonian exile was used by Martin Luther who argued that the gospel had been exiled in his time by the Babylonian captivity of the Roman Catholic Church.[2] Thus he intended exile to be a very harsh metaphor to suggest that the shaping influence of the Roman Catholic Church of his time was alien and hostile to the gospel. We do not need to pursue Luther's particular handling of the metaphor to see its potential for our own interpretive situation.[3]

As we try to appropriate the metaphor of exile, we may wish to think about the church and ask if we are in exile. The metaphor of exile may be useful to American Christians as a way of understanding the social context of the church in American culture. The exile of the contemporary American church is that we are bombarded by definitions of reality that are fundamentally alien to the gospel, definitions of reality that come from the military-industrial-scientific empire, which may be characterized as "consumer capitalism."[4] In a variety of ways the voice of this empire wants to reshape our values, fears, and dreams in ways that are fundamentally opposed to the voice of the gospel.

There are, of course, many American Christians who do not know this and do not believe it. It is not known or believed because they sense no abrasion between those cultural values and evangelical values (values derived from the gospel). Such American Christians proceed on the assumption that our society is fundamentally Christian and that there is a ready and comfortable interface between Christianity and those cultural values. If that view be held (which I think is wrong), then the exilic literature makes little sense or has no direct pertinence. That is an important issue for the way in which our argument proceeds. If the church is in fact in exile, as I believe it to be, then to try to do ministry as if we are practicing imperial religion robs us of energy. My own judgment is that honestly facing exile as our real situation generates energy for imaginative and faithful living. Exile in the ancient world or in our own situation is not an obvious, flat, social fact. It is a decision one must make. It is a very specific, self-conscious reading of social reality. There must have been many Jews in Babylon in the sixth century who settled in, made it home, assimilated, and did not perceive themselves as exiles. Such accommodation is a possible stance for faith, in ancient Babylon or in contemporary America. I should only say that such a pragmatic decision against exile excludes one from the imaginative field of this literature of exile. "Exile" is not simply a geographical fact, but also a theological decision.

My interpretive analogue from 2 Isaiah is aimed at the American situation, where I find the claims of the gospel not hospitably received. One can make the same exilic reading of the church community in the totalitarian context of Eastern Europe. Quite clearly, the church there is a community in an alien and hostile environment. I do not propose the church context of Eastern Europe as a preferable alternative to our own, for the gospel is rejected by the dominant values there as well. But I suggest our task as pastors and Christians is not to use our energy on those more distant issues but to face the faith situation of exile as it concerns us where our ministry is given. Our American faith situation may be more seductive than such oppressive contexts because the reading of exile is not so unambiguous for us. I proceed here, however, on the assumption that the notion of the Christian church in American culture being in exile is a correct reading of the situation. I do so strategically in order to make a case from this literature. I do so because that is in fact my assessment of our social situation. In the argument that follows, then, I assume that our situation as

American Christians may be treated as a very rough parallel to that of Jews in the Babylonian empire. In both the Babylonian and American contexts, there are many dimensions of life to be affirmed and appropriated. But in both the fundamental perceptions and values are in opposition to the faith of Israel.

Second Isaiah's poetry is organized around the metaphor of homecoming, a metaphor that makes sense only to those who read their context as exile. The whole of this poetry is preoccupied with one overriding proclamation: *homecoming*. Thus Isaiah 40:1–11 envisions a great procession led by Yahweh as exiled Jews come home. Yahweh will gather into the land of Zion all those who had been scattered in exile (43:5–6). The watchmen on the walls of desolate Jerusalem watch with eager longing for some news of a fresh possibility. When they receive word of Yahweh's triumphant return from exile, they rejoice (52:7–10). As a result, the fallen city will be rebuilt (44:28; 54:11–12). There will be a rebuilding and a gathering (49:17–18). Judah had been hopeless but now will be safely at home. It is for this reason that new songs of joy, celebration, and buoyancy can now be sung (42:10–17).

By the power and the mercy of God, this community of faith will very soon be led back to the "holy land" where the values of the Torah tradition are not resisted but in fact received and practiced as normative and true. It is a deep yearning in this faith community of exile to be in the only place where those values are presumed. For good reason that place is "home."

The use of these two metaphors, *exile* and *homecoming*, is an act of remarkable evangelical imagination. The *homecoming* metaphor makes sense only where the metaphor of *exile* has been accepted as true. Second Isaiah's poetry of homecoming is precisely imaginative poetry which liberates. It is not based in political analysis, though the poet obviously knew what was going on in his world. It is an imaginative act of speech that intends to evoke reality and lead this community out beyond their present situation. The poetry is grounded in a theological conviction of God's sovereignty (40:9–11; 52:7). It is also informed by political analysis (45:1–6). The poetry, as such, is not explained either by theological conviction or by political analysis, but by an inventive, creative act of poetry that means to speak this community out beyond present circumstance by the force of the poetic word, which is offered as the fresh decree of God's own mouth (46:11;

55:10–11). I am assuming that the power of language to shape reality and not just describe reality is true for us as well as for this poet. The poet does not only describe a new social reality but wills it. The very art of poetic speech establishes new reality. Public speech, the articulation of alternative scenarios of reality, is one of the key acts of a ministry among exiles.[5]

The exiles were securely and perhaps despondently exiles. They could not imagine any other status. They accepted Babylonian definitions of reality, not because they were convinced, but because no alternatives were available. These Babylonian claims seemed as if they would endure to perpetuity (47:7, 8, 10). This exiled community was in despair because it accepted Babylonian definitions of reality and did not know any others were available. That is, they were hopeless. They did not believe Yahweh could counter Babylon (49:14; 50:2).

It was the peculiar vocation of 2 Isaiah to construct poetic scenarios of alternative reality outside the prosaic control of the empire. These fresh alternatives liberated Jewish exiles to think differently, act differently, speak differently, and sing differently. In the end Babylonian definitions of reality lost their absoluteness and their authority because this poetry served to subvert the absoluteness.

The Babylonian gods have been dethroned by the poetry:

> Bel bows down, Nebo stoops . . .
> They stoop, they bow down together,
>   they cannot save the burden,
>   but themselves go into captivity. (Isa. 46:1–2)

The very gods who authorized captivity for Judah are now themselves destined to the same fate. As the gods are subverted in this poetry, so the inflated claims of the empire are also emptied in humiliation:

> Come down and sit in the dust,
>   O virgin daughter of Babylon;
> sit on the ground without a throne,
>   O daughter of the Chaldeans! (Isa. 47:1)

The poetry articulates an empire that has failed and is humiliated. It need no longer be feared or trusted. Freedom to go home began to well up in this community. The poet offers scenarios of a triumphant procession on its way home in joy and power (40:1–11; 43:4–7; 45:14–17).

The triggering of this new social possibility is a poetic articulation of an alternative social reality that at first lives only in the mind and heart of the poet but begins to form a community ready in various ways to disengage from the dominant reality. That was the ministry of this poet in exile. Our ministry in our exile requires the same clarity and courage that 2 Isaiah had which gave energy and freedom in his exile.

IMAGINATION TOWARD WHAT WILL BE

The practice of such *poetic imagination* is the most subversive, redemptive act that a leader of a faith community can undertake in the midst of exiles. This work of poetic alternative in the long run is more crucial than one-on-one pastoral care or the careful implementation of institutional goals. That is because the work of poetic imagination holds the potential of unleashing a community of power and action that finally will not be contained by any imperial restrictions and definitions of reality.

1. Second Isaiah is the supreme example of liberated poetic imagination in the Old Testament. We are so familiar with the words that we fail to note how the poetic rendering evokes an entirely different perception of reality. The poetry is not derived from external historical experience. The poetry cannot be adequately explained by observing that Babylonian power would eventually succumb to the rise of Persia under Cyrus. Poetry here is not simply code language for political events.

Rather, the poet appeals to the old memories and affirmations in an astonishing way to jar the perceptual field of Israel and to cause a wholly new discernment of reality. The poetry opens with a heavenly scenario in which the voices of members of the divine council fashion a new proclamation (40:1-8). This is immediately followed by a rhetorical act of enthronement (40:9) in which Yahweh, who had seemed weak, is now placed triumphantly at the head of a grand procession (40:10-11).

The poetry does not describe what is happening. Rather it evokes images and invites perceptions in Israel that were not available apart from this poetry. The poetry is not aimed first of all at external conduct, as though the poet expected people immediately to start packing for travel. Rather, the poetry cuts underneath behavior to begin to transform the self-image, communal image, and image of historical possibility. The rhetoric works to deabsolutize imperial modes of reality, so that fresh forms of communal possibility can be entertained. Second Isaiah's dramatic sensitivity constructs worlds of gods in court (41:21-29), rulers being summoned by Yahweh (44:24-28; 45:1-5), dragons being defeated (51:9), cities being rebuilt (54:11-14). The outcome of such poetry is hope. It is hope which makes community possible on the way out of the empire.

The poet creates with incredible scope and vividness. One can hear the chains rattling and the nations yielding. One can conjure Cyrus acting in liberation and Babylonians cowering in subjugation. One can hear the ecstatic sounds of Sarah now with child (54:1-3), and the flood waters of Noah subsiding (54:9-11).

2. Jesus' way of teaching through parables was such a pastoral act of prophetic imagination in which he invited his community of listeners out beyond the visible realities of Roman law and the ways in which Jewish law had grown restrictive in his time.[6] Like 2 Isaiah, Jesus does this precisely out of the tradition itself. It is clear that he tells parables consistent with the rabbinic tradition, but his parables serve to conjure alternative social reality. They are specific, but they are open-ended. The listener, when the story is ended, is not instructed and does not know what to do. The stories intend to characterize an alternative society which he calls "kingdom of God,"[7] but the stories do not offer blueprints, budgets, or programs. They only tease the listeners to begin to turn loose of the givens of the day and to live toward a new social possibility. The parables of Jesus clearly undermine the dominant social reality of his day. In fact, Jesus invites his listeners to a homecoming, for he insists that this kingdom is in fact one's true home. Every other place, no matter where, is a place of exile and alienation. That is why we know about "restless hearts" and "social unrest." These stories are an offer of genuine rest, at home.

3. The most compelling example of this imaginative articulation of an alternative in American culture may be in the liberated preaching of the black church. The best-known case, of course, is Martin Luther King, Jr. We ought not to miss the power of his language. He no doubt was a master politician and a social strategist and an adept man-

ager of the media, but first and best, he had the tongue of a poet and the cadence of liberty in his speech. He was able to summon an exiled community out beyond the imperial definitions of the day which held his people in bondage. When he issued his famous poetic proposal, "I have a dream," that was just such a summons.[8] He did not have a concrete notion on how to enact that dream, but it was a beginning point of energy. The dream functioned as an act of incredible hope, but it was also an act of heavy critique which asserted that the present social reality is not working. It was an announcement that things would not stay as they were (cf. Isa. 43:18–19).

Out of the daring poetry of liberated black imagination, social reality began to crack open and homecoming became possible. The social reality that had seemed to be eternally ordained now appeared to be only a doubtful social contrivance. Second Isaiah's mockery of the gods serves the same end as did the dreaming of Martin Luther King, Jr. (cf. 41:21–29):

The poetry of 2 Isaiah dreams of homecoming and begins to nullify Babylonian definitions of reality.

The parables of Jesus initiate dreams of homecoming and begin to subvert the oppressive social institutions and presuppositions of his day.

The oracles of Martin Luther King, Jr., dance about Stone Mountain and begin to cause trembling in the racist structures of the day.

All three of these poetic acts are models of liberated, liberating speech that stands in sharp contrast to our conventional domesticated speech. We mostly are scribes maintaining the order of the day. We mostly are appreciated by and paid by people who like it the way it is, who do not sense our exile and resist discerning it, who do not yearn for a homecoming because we have fooled ourselves into thinking this present arrangement is our home. To accommodate such social reality, our language becomes prosaic and didactic, because it helps keep the lid on things. Our language becomes descriptive, because it is better to tell *what is,* than to trust *what will be.* Our church talk becomes dull and contained as all other talk in such a flat imperial society as ours.

Such a flattened tongue permits no vitality in ministry. Consider the phrase, "freedom of the pulpit." That phrase does not mean a license so that the minister can say any fool thing he or she wants. Rather it means that we are agreed that what is said here is to be said out of the power and freedom and affront of the gospel, without accommodating the conventions of the day. The pulpit—the speech practice of the church—is the place for imaginative speech that does not conform to the economic interests, moral limits, or epistemological convictions of the dominant culture.[9] Such speech is not imperative or exhortative or coercive. It tells no one what to do, but it redescribes the world so that Babylon, which looked so benign, is now seen as exile, so that Palestine, which was loved and lost, now looks like home, so that we who looked like docile slaves are on our way rejoicing. The central task of ministry is the formation of a community with an alternative, liberated imagination that has the courage and the freedom to act in a different vision and a different perception of reality.

Two reference points are available for such a new way of speech. On the one hand, it is the text and the tradition which give us the materials for new metaphors. On the other hand, it is the present reality of pain which energizes and illuminates the metaphors. It is the interaction of remembered text and present pain that form the matrix out of which comes new speech. It is clear that 2 Isaiah's poetry is precisely such an interaction of text and pain.

THE UNFETTERED POWER OF THE WORD

Second Isaiah has remarkable things to say to his contemporaries that have no point of reference in domesticated reality. What he says is not derived from his Babylonian experience. His poetry is indeed about the powerful overriding word of God which will finally have its say in history (Isa. 40:6-8; 55:10-11). This theology of the word refers to a sense that there is an indefatigable agency at work in the historical process that takes its own free course and has its decisive say without conforming to the power and processes of the day. The God who is the subject of the word is also the subject of transformative action in the experience of Israel. The tradition of Isaiah in its early rootage had insisted that Yahweh's decree is more powerful that alien empires (cf. Isa. 14:24-27; 37:26-29). That word is rooted in God's primal intention, but it comes to fruition in concrete historical experience. As Yahweh had created the world by decree (Genesis 1; Ps. 33:4-9), so the history of the Near East and the life of Israel begins again by that same speech.

Scholars have long noted that the poetry of 2 Isaiah is bounded by "the word." At the beginning in 40:8:

> The grass withers, the flower fades;
> but *the word of our God* will stand for ever.

The grass presumably refers to the pretensions of the Babylonian empire. That empire, contrary to appearances, is incredibly transitory and not to be feared or respected. The purpose of God will outlast the empire and all of its posturing (cf. the metaphor in Pss. 90:5–6; 103:15–16). At the conclusion of the corpus, the poet returns to the theme:

> So shall *my word* be that goes forth from my mouth.
> It shall not return to me empty,
> but it shall accomplish that which I propose. (Isa. 55:11; au. trans.)

The promise of God over the historical process cannot be defeated.

The word of the word is utilized negatively concerning false gods who can speak no word. The lawsuit form of Isa. 41:22–23 taunts the other gods. They are challenged to speak: "tell us . . . tell us . . . declare . . . tell us." But there is a long silence in heaven, because the other gods are mute and dumb (cf. Isa. 44:18; Ps. 115:5–7). Speech is power. To have power, a god must speak. Such speech must be a serious decree that causes something to happen. But Babylonian gods are silent, have no word to speak, because they can cause nothing.

By contrast Yahweh is a God who speaks, whose word is effective and whose decree is carried out in the world. In 55:10–11, the speech of Yahweh is not futile. Yahweh does what Yahweh says (46:11). Yahweh must therefore be taken more seriously than the Babylonian gods. What Yahweh speaks is the fall of Babylon and the corresponding liberation of Israel. The same word that frees Israel is the word that creates worlds. Thus 55:12–13 envisions a transformation of creation, the inversion of Gen. 3:18. The word will transform both creation and imperial history. That speech permits Israel to go home.

That transformative word is an incredible promise asserted against the reality of the empire. God's way in the world may use Babylon (Jer. 25:9; 27:6), even as it used Assyria (Isa. 10:5–19), and subsequently will use Persia (Isa. 45:1). But the purposes of Yahweh are never controlled by the empire. Everything for this poet hinges on Yahweh's sovereign freedom, first to use Babylon, and then to dispose of Babylon, without regret or reservation. Yahweh uses and disposes of empires to work his decree in relation to this exiled people. The decree prevails. Empires come and go in relation to it. It is that sovereign word that comes to fleshly reality in the coming of Cyrus (44:24-28). It is the word (v. 26) which culminates in Cyrus (v. 28).

The contrast between the powerful purpose of God and the claims of the empire is articulated in the familiar words:

> My plans are not your plans,
>   neither are your ways my ways, says the Lord,
> For as the heavens are higher than the earth,
>   so are my ways higher than your ways,
>   and my plans than your plans. (Isa. 55:8-9; au. trans.)

This is not some kind of mysterious transcendentalism. It is rather a claim that purposes coming to realization are in fact the purposes of God and not those of Babylon (cf. 14:24-27). Indeed the voices of Babylonian power are mute and inconsequential (41:21-23, 26), not to be trusted or feared.

The claims of an overriding purpose from Yahweh will be difficult for us. We are all children of modernity. We take things as we see them. We do not credit easily the claims of poetry that are against the hardware of the day. It is hard to trust poetry more than custom hardware. That no doubt is a problem for us moderns, but it is not exclusively a modern problem. Every imperial agent wants to reduce what is possible to what is available.[10] No doubt this poetic insistence was difficult the first time it was uttered, because it was against the presumed data of the situation. The claim was not obvious then. It was only obvious to this poet who had uncommon, unfettered imagination. His capacity was to set in motion a new historical venture that changed the shape of Judah's history. But the change began in his liberated, imaginative speech about the overriding purpose of God in the process.

MEMORIES WITH A FUTURE

Like Ezekiel before him, this poet is deeply rooted in the tradition.[11]

Imagination is not a freelance, ad hoc operation that spins out novelty. Imagination, of the kind we are speaking, is a fresh, liberated return to the memory. When 2 Isaiah returns to the memory, he reads the tradition for his own moment, even as did Ezekiel for his. But because the situation is different, the anticipatory outcome of the tradition is also very different. Whereas Ezekiel read the memory as a statement of judgment and rebuke, 2 Isaiah reads it as a new gift. He does not regard the past as a closed record, but as a force that still keeps offering its gifts.

Abraham and Sarah (51:2-3) become a point of reference for the comfort of exiled Judah that are seen not to be without hope.[12]

Barren Sarah (54:1-3) becomes the fruitful mother of a whole new community. Her children, like those of the ancient midwives (Exod. 1:15-22), will outnumber the children of the empire.

Noah (54:9-11) becomes the model for the announcement of steadfast love, for the exile is like a chaotic flood and it is to end in peace and compassion.

David (55:3) becomes the root of a new covenant made to the whole community.[13] As David lived out of the promise, so the whole community can now live out of the promise.

To find in the memory such power for the present and for the future requires free sensitivity and intergenerational identity. It requires a break with the kind of imperial individualism that believes all the promises must be given to me, now. It takes courage to explore the memory, especially in a situation of amnesia like ours. Perhaps the community of the poet has no memory, for the empire insists that particularistic communities forget their particular rootage for the sake of universal myths. The particulars are such an embarrassment to the regime. People who believe the universal myths are easier to administer, for then we are all alike and indeed we are really replaceable parts. It is not different among us. When we have completely forgotten our past, we will absolutize the present and we will be like contented cows in Bashan who want nothing more than the best of today. People like that can never remember who they are, cannot remember their status as exiles or that home is somewhere else. It takes a powerful articulation of memory to maintain a sense of identity in the midst of exile.

THE POET AS PASTOR

This poet operates with incredible pastoral sensitivity. He wants his community to think afresh, decide afresh, and act freely. He knows that this is a terrifying possibility. We are frightened nearly to death to run any risks, to stand out in the crowd, to go against conventional opinion. Who knows? If one criticizes the Babylonian arrangement, one might lose a job or a place in the university. The poet, for that reason, is present as a pastor, to nurture, nudge, and reassure about the little moves of liberated identity. Not many of us make big moves, only little moves. Even these scare us.

This nurturing of counterconsciousness is best expressed in the salvation oracles (41:8–14; 43:1–5; 44:1–4), which counter the fear and intimidation with a "fear not."[14] To utter the assurance is to recognize the fear. It is to read it as normal and without reprimand, but it is also to respond to it, to deal with it, to overcome it. The salvation oracle is an assurance of solidarity.

The form appears to have rootage in the old war traditions of Yahwism which assured Yahweh's presence with and commitment to Israel in the midst of military danger (cf. Exod. 14:13; Deut. 20:3–4). The form is used in this poetry to reassure exilic Israel that Yahweh's presence and solidarity with Israel more than offsets the threat and reality of Babylon:

> Fear not, for I am with you,
>   be not dismayed, for I am your God. (41:10)

> Fear not, you worm Jacob,
>   you men of Israel!
> I will help you, says the Lord;
>   your Redeemer is the Holy One of Israel. (41:14)

> Fear not, for I have redeemed you;
>   I have called you by name, you are mine.
> When you pass through the waters
>   I will be with you,
>   and through the rivers, they shall not overwhelm you. (43:1–2)

When you pass through the waters, through the danger point, through the police station, through the customs office, when you are called to give an account of your new identity, you will not be there alone. The assurance, in the form it is cast in Isa. 43:1-5, is an announcement that sounds like a baptismal formula: "I have called you by name, you are mine." You belong to the hopes and memories of Yahwism. You do not belong to Babylon. You are mine, not theirs. Such a liturgical formula is not worth much unless it comes with an act of concrete solidarity, which presumably it did. This rhetorical act of solidarity is a life-changing assertion because it begins to dismantle the conventional assumption that Babylon is the only game in town. Think what kind of imagination it would take to envision and articulate an alternative identity! Such imagination is evident in the claim of salvation oracles in the midst of the empire. It is also evident in the claim of baptismal reassurance in the midst of an alien culture.

The intimate pastoral "fear not" is matched in this poetry by an imaginative assertion, no doubt acted out in liturgy, of the enthronement of Yahweh. The poet invites the community to a scenario in which the gods are on trial.

The other gods are invited to testify on their own behalf:

> Set forth your case, says the Lord;
> bring your proofs, says the King of Jacob.
> Let them bring them and tell us
> what is to happen.
> Tell us the former things, what they are,
> that we may consider them,
> that we may know their outcome;
> or declare to us the things to come.
> Tell us what is to come hereafter,
> that we may know that you are gods;
> do good, or do harm,
> that we may be dismayed and terrified. (41:21-23)

But of course they cannot:

> Behold, you are nothing,
> and your work is nought;
> an abomination is he who chooses you. (42:24)

The contrast is complete for Yahweh can and does speak effectively:

> I stirred up one from the north, and he has come,
> from the rising of the sun, and he shall call on my name;

> he shall trample on rulers as on mortar,
>   as the potter treads clay.
> Who declared it from the beginning, that we might know,
>   and beforetime, that we might say, "He is right"?
> There was none who declared it, none who proclaimed,
>   none who heard your words.
> I first have declared it to Zion,
>   and I give to Jerusalem a herald of good tidings. (41:25–27)

Yahweh speaks because he has something to say about his powerful decrees that change historical reality. The function of this rhetoric is to contrast Yahweh and the gods, to distance Yahweh from imperial reality, to assert Yahweh's incomparability. But the theological intent is to delegitimate and dismiss the other gods, thereby overthrowing the imaginative, symbolic power of coercion practiced by the empire. By creating space for celebration of Yahweh, the poet creates space for liberated action. Freedom against Babylon is rooted in the liturgical assertion of Yahweh's unchallengeable governance.

The poet asserts the contrast in most absolute categories:

> God is with you only, and there is no other,
>   no god besides him. (45:14)

> To whom will you liken me and make me equal,
>   and compare me, that we may be alike? (46:5)

> My glory I will not give to another. (48:11; cf. 42:8)

It is as though one were to juxtapose the God of the gospel with the gods of consumer capitalism, just as the old liturgy has contrasted the God of Moses and the gods of the Pharaoh (Exodus 5—10). The liturgy becomes a trial scene, in which each god is invited to give evidence of its authority, its power, its capacity to get things done, its ability to keep its promises.

The gods of Babylon have seemed so beyond reach, to be presumed and eternally taken for granted. But that is because no one had posed a serious question. Now this poet has the courage to ask, to look more closely, to inquire, "When was the last time a Babylonian god did anything that mattered for our well-being?" It turns out that the gods of the empire are a fraud, much noise and no substance, not able to make any difference at all. This other God, the one named in the tradition of Israel (Exod. 3:14) is shown by this poet to be the real one, the one with power to be trusted, even toward homecoming (45:21). Now again, notice the imaginative act of this remarkable poetry. Second Isaiah's reading of reality was not evident on the face of it. Jewish life in Babylon could have been read differently. It is an act of poetic courage that this poet is able to shape the perception of the community in a very special way, to read reality from the point of view of exile and homecoming, to reject every imperial reading. The outcome of the poetry—and it is only poetry and not a political proposal—is that the gods of Babylon are to be laughed at because they cannot in fact make any difference (41:21–24). Israel thus is freed to think differently about its own future and its loyalties. The competing loyalties that float around this community are named and assessed, the one to truth and validity, the other to falseness and emptiness. This partisan poetry stares the community in the face and waits. It requires a decision.

NEW WORLD POETRY

The authority for this staggering and subversive poetry that assaults the empire and creates space and courage for Israelite praxis is founded in the initial assertion of Isa. 40:1–11. It is this passage, frequently reckoned as a "call narrative," which asserts the authority upon which the poetry is based.[15] The dialogue of that text concerns the commissioning of the poet by the divine council.[16] The poet portrays a conversation in the divine council that authorizes the poet to articulate an alternative vision of social reality (compare 1 Kings 22:19–23).

The one commissioned is authorized to speak Yahweh's sovereign word of power, which is contrasted with the failed word of the empire: "the grassy empire withers, the word abides" (vv. 6–8).

In the face of pretenders to real power, Yahweh is asserted as the real king who must be acknowledged (v. 9; cf. 52:7). The formula, "behold your God," probably borrowed from the liturgy of enthronement, announces a new governance which destabilizes all would-be rulers.

On the basis of this alternative governance acted out in a liturgy of enthronement, the poet dares to announce the imperative, "comfort, comfort" (40:1).

To comfort genuinely hopeless people who have flattened futures is not easy business. This kind of language functions as exile-ending speech. It is the announcement that homecoming is possible. But what does it mean to comfort? It does not mean to assure people it is all right to accept the imperial regime. If they wanted such an assurance, they would not have come to this poet. Rather, it means to give people permission to see the exile for what it is and to begin to move home.

The summons of this poet is not to express religious poetry. It is to shape communal imagination so that its true situation can be discerned. People cannot operate in new ways unless they are able to see afresh their real cultural circumstance. A new circumstance is brought vigorously to speech by this poet:

Israel is invited to sing a new song to celebrate a new regime. The new song is to replace the anthem of the empire (42:10).

This poetic speech debunks Babylonian gods and makes them objects of scorn (46:1-2).

This speech dismantles Babylonian power which had become autonomous (47).

This speech invites Israel to eat different bread (55:1-3), not the bread of the Herodians and the Pharisees (Mark 8:15), not the bread of the empire (cf. Dan. 1) which does not nourish, but new free bread.

Every aspect of this community is invited to a new orientation.

The new orientation wrought by poetry out of memory through liturgy consists in rereading reality through three metaphors:

Exile is a sense of not belonging, of being in an environment hostile to the values of this community and its vocation. Exile is practiced among those who refuse to accept and be assimilated in the new situation. Psalm 137 is a passionate resolve not to be assimilated. The poetry of 2 Isaiah in turn is a summons away from such assimilation.

Babylon refers to a concentration of power and value which is dominant and which is finally hostile to the covenant faith of this community. The empire regularly seeks to domesticate such a community with a special vocation and characteristically ends in oppression.

Homecoming is a dramatic decision to break with imperial rationality and to embrace a place called home where covenantal values have currency and credibility.

The juxtaposition of exile, Babylon, and homecoming means that this poetry of 2 Isaiah is not aimed simply at geographical, spatial possibility but at a relational, covenantal reality. The poetry permits a very different reading of social reality, opening up quite new social possibilities. The poetry evokes the sense that the world can and will be organized differently. Only a poet could make available such a drastically subversive conviction and invitation.

6

"SING, O BARREN ONE"

(ISAIAH 54:1–17)

SECOND ISAIAH LIVES at the other side of the exile, as the signs accumulate that there will be a homecoming.[1] Clearly the mood has changed. The anguish of Jeremiah and the heaviness of Ezekiel have been established as reality and do not need to be reiterated or doubted. This is a new generation. A new word needs to be spoken to it, yet that new word does not nullify or retract anything that came before.

Whatever that new word is, it must be spoken in a Babylonian context. Jeremiah is the one who programmatically announced that Babylonian reality was to be the great new fact of Israel. God has sent "my servant Nebuchadnezzar" (25:9; 27:6) to destroy this recalcitrant Israel. Resistance to Babylon was equated by Jeremiah with resistance to the history-making purposes of Yahweh.

After the first deportation of 598, Jeremiah and Ezekiel had developed a second theme. Not only is Babylon the agent of God's destruction. Babylon is also to be the habitat for faithful Israel. This is an extraordinary judgment (made in Jeremiah 24; Ezekiel 11) which announces that the community of Jewish exiles in Babylon who obviously were the displaced ones are in fact God's special people who are the wave of the future for Judaism.[2] The displaced ones are to become the faithful ones and finally the blessed ones. In part that may be a historical, sociological judgment, because this group contained the professional element that must lead Judaism if there is to be a future. In part

109

the decision is an act of propaganda made for ideological reasons. That is, it surely must be a self-serving, partisan statement by the exiles themselves announcing their own special, chosen status. But biblical faith (and the historical process) have accepted that partisan claim as theologically correct and historically accurate, even if its origins are in propaganda. Whatever future there is will come out of Babylon, for the empire will not finally prevail (cf. Jeremiah 51—52).

Babylon has been the great enemy and threat. But two generations later, in the time of 2 Isaiah, the imperial threat had become the great seduction. Babylon had become home. Jeremiah had urged that (29:5-7), and it had happened. These Jewish families and community had now been in Babylon for two generations. They had entered into the public life of Babylon, with some economic successes, no doubt with educational and cultural attachments. Jewish rootage and identity were still significant. There was still a general liturgical longing for Jerusalem. But such a general liturgical longing is not easily translated into the concrete act of going back home from the relative security of a well-defined Babylonian situation to the shabby, chancy Judean situation.

THE REJECTION OF A FALSE HOME

Second Isaiah addresses Babylonian Jews about *going home*, but that is not quite adequate. His community, of course, consisted in Babylonian Jews. But his powerful poetry wants, through the mediation of metaphor, to assert a more specific and intense identity for this community, namely *exile*. The metaphor of exile, I submit, is more important for this literature than is the geohistorical fact of Babylon. The notion of exile is a rather peculiar one.

In the first instance, exile is *geographical*. "Exile" means to be deported, displaced, transplanted. It is to end up in a strange setting. But more than this, exile is an intentional identity that is *theological* as well as geographical. "Exile" articulates that the new place is not home and can never be home because its realities are essentially alien and inhospitable to our true theological identity. Now I suggest that accepting identity as an exile, along with geographical reality, is an act of polemical theological imagination that guards against cultural assimilation. Exiles have a stake in stating clearly, perhaps in exaggerated form, the differences between the identity and faith of the community and the seductive urgings and promises of the empire.

The central task of 2 Isaiah is to invite people home, to create a sense of that prospect and hope. But in order to do that, the poet had to convert Babylonian Jews into exiles, to persuade displaced people that after two generations, this is still not home. The theological attractiveness of home in Jerusalem had to be stated against the social, economic, and political benefits of Babylon, which felt more concretely like home. Second Isaiah's task is a play of imagination against the immediate visible reality, a difficult task indeed.

Because exile is a theological issue as distinct from a geographical issue, 2 Isaiah has to make the case for both exile and homecoming on theological grounds. That is, he has to assert by doxology and argue by polemic that the God of Israel is the true, powerful, faithful God who can be trusted in this journey home. He has to argue that the gods of Babylon are in fact neither powerful nor faithful and are not to be trusted or feared. The claims of theological reality thus fly in the face of imperial reality, because against Israel's faith affirmation, the Babylonian gods seemed to have delivered the goods.

The argument for trust in Yahweh is mounted by 2 Isaiah in two basic ways. The first is a series of salvation oracles,[3] which assure Jews that God is with them and they need not fear. God is indeed faithful and concerned for Israel.

The second way of articulating trust in Yahweh is the lawsuit form which dramatizes the juridical contest between Yahweh and the other gods.[4] Whereas Yahweh, it is asserted, speaks a powerful word (cf. Isa. 40:8; 55:10-11) that controls history, the Babylonian gods are sarcastically shown to be mute and therefore irrelevant and obsolete, because they cannot change history (41:22-24, 28-29). The grand claim for Yahweh made with poetic courage is that Yahweh has authorized and summoned Cyrus the Persian king who in this very moment is assaulting and destroying the Babylonian empire (44:24-28; 45:1).

The political outcome of this dramatic argument, as the poetry of 2 Isaiah unfolds, is that the Babylonian gods (Isa. 46:1-2) and the Babylonian regime (47:1-15) are debunked. Israel is invited to withdraw its allegiance from an empire that has now been exposed theologically and poetically as illegitimate and dysfunctional. If Jews can make that imaginative withdrawal, they may indeed withdraw from Babylonian reality, Babylonian rationality, Babylonian fears and hopes, and be open to the reality, rationality, fears, and hopes that are properly their own as Jews. If that imaginative transference can be established, then the actual geopolitical move can be made. If that imaginative, liturgical scenario is not credible, then the geographical uprooting entailed in going home is unlikely. Everything depends on this imaginative presentation of an alternative scenario that makes a contrast among the gods. When the gods are clearly contrasted, that contrast has important implications for relations between the nations.

POETRY AUTHORIZED BY MEMORY

The question for Israel and for the poet of 2 Isaiah is, why should the radical imagination of this poetry be trusted and acted upon? The answer to that, which I consider here, is that memory is the only ground which makes an alternative scenario to the empire credible. The empire, Babylonian or any other, wants to establish itself as absolute, wants the present arrangement to appear eternal in the past as in the future, so that after a while, one cannot remember when it was different from this, which means having available to our imagination no real alternative.

Against such imperial absoluteness and positivism, memory can be a keenly subversive activity. It is the community hosting in its imagination a tale of how it was back before the empire, before this particular set of hopes and fears gained hegemony. This alternative tale is a threat to the empire because it asserts not only that it used to be different in the past but that it could be different in the future. For this situation, the Israelite Torah tradition is a threat to Babylonian claims, because in that narrative and its liturgical enactments, another history is made available, a history governed in different ways by this very different God, Yahweh, who has no imperial ambition or pretension.

It is plausible to imagine that Babylon wanted to silence this memory, because such future-giving memory is the main thing an established empire has to fear. That is why empires fear books and poets. It is also plausible that this historical memory of an Israelite alternative was an awkward embarrassment to assimilated Jews who had succeeded in the imperial world and did not want their children handicapped by such a phenomenon.

The poem of 2 Isaiah proceeds as an act of passion, an act of obedience, an act of hope, an act of subversion. The memory about which we are speaking is a quite specific one, the narrative memory of Israel, which is articulated in concise credo, in liberated song and poetry, in liturgical recital and in the more expansive, reflective literature of the Torah. This is the memory of quite specific and familiar content which has taken shape from the concrete experience of Israel. That concrete memory has been stylized in paradigmatic ways to function as canon. This memory is the life-giving inheritance that the older generation has to give to the younger (cf. Ps. 78:1–8).[5]

This memory is articulated in two quite different ways.[6] On the one hand, derivative from Moses, there is the tradition of protest and demand (Exodus and Sinai) through which each new generation is summoned to a radical engagement with the demands of Yahweh. Because this memory concerns obedience and summons, it is a tradition of immediacy which presents an either/or. This tradition is used by 2 Isaiah (see Isa. 43:18–19).[7] However, it is used in 2 Isaiah (cf. also Jer. 23:7–8) not as a tradition which endures and sustains but as a tradition which models, evokes, and legitimates a newness marked by amazement and discontinuity. This tradition is used by 2 Isaiah as a type to illuminate what is immediately present in the contemporary experience of Israel. The memory of Exodus illuminates the "new thing" of the poem. This Mosaic tradition by itself, however, does not provide the buoyancy and continuity needed for exiles.

On the other hand, there is a second kind of memory used by 2 Isaiah to which we will attend in more detail. Unlike the memories rooted in Moses, these memories concern continuity, durability, and consolidation. They do not speak of an old event that only illuminates the present but of an old event which continues to be present amid current experience. These memories, with a kind of reliable density, intrude out of the past into the present and so change the present. Most important, these memories of durability and continuity include the tradition of Abraham and Sarah, less centrally the memories of Noah and David. These memories are used to affirm that there is more present in this experience than the imperial agents of Babylon suspect. It is that 'more' that gives life and power to Israel in exile.

It is surprising that in a moment of acute communal possibility matched by a poignant moment in the empire (the threat of Cyrus), 2 Isaiah spends his time on memory. One might have guessed the poet had other, more important things to do. He might have been engaged more directly in pastoral issues with frightened, bewildered people. He might have better used his time with educating the new generation into the vocation of this community. He might have better engaged in political conversation and strategy sessions. In some ways the text is about all of these tasks, but not in any direct way. Second Isaiah had decided that in this moment of energizing and poignancy, his most important work was to process the memory, to engage in the traditioning task, to be sure that the present is reread in light of this quite distinctive memory.

To understand why 2 Isaiah may have made this important decision about priorities, we consider the "possibility" element of "Only Memory Allows Possibility." I submit that this poet engaged the memory in order to address the issue of possibility. I am using the term in a specifically Israelite way which is not to be confused with "possibility thinking." As I understand it, the word is rooted particularly in Gen. 18:1–15 in which the question is posed, "Is anything impossible for God?"[8] Here "possibility" does not refer to human possibility. The narrative does not ask what is possible for Sarah or for Abraham. Rather, it enquires about what is possible for God. The import of the narrative is that the freedom, power, and sovereignty of Yahweh make possible precisely what the world regards as impossible. The question in Gen. 18:14 lingers in the memory of Israel and waits for each new generation to give answer, even until the answer of Jesus (Mark 10:27; 14:36).

Second Isaiah and his contemporaries lived in an imperial situation in which the Babylonians tightly defined what is possible and permissable. What is clearly not possible is the freedom to go home. A Jewish homecoming is impossible in the face of Babylonian policy and definitions of reality. The purpose of the poetry of 2 Isaiah is to announce the possibility of homecoming even though the empire declared it impossible. That is, the pastoral task is to move the imagination of this community beyond imperial parameters to assert that what the empire holds to be impossible is precisely possible through the liberating will of Yahweh.

The issue then is this: How can one assert that something which the empire judges to be impossible is possible for God? The answer is found in the memory.[9] The memory makes available to Israel in exile models, paradigms, and concrete references about old impossibilities which linger with power. The tale of Sarah and Abraham thus is told as a memory which continues to be actualized and fulfilled in this time in Israel's life. The power of this memory of impossibility works its transformative, subversive effect in the imagination of the present generation. Clearly only this memory, powerfully and passionately made available, prevents acceptance of imperial decisions about what is possible.

FROM MEMORY TO HISTORICAL POSSIBILITY

The text we consider is Isa. 54:1–17. We will focus on vv. 1–10. Prior to this poem, the poet has assaulted and dismantled both the gods and the political apparatus of the empire (46:1–2; 47:1–15). That is, he has done the dismantling that can be done by rhetoric. His intent is to create space in which Israel can see that the claims of the empire are now void, thus permitting and requiring new action.

But even when the call for external realities to be changed is given, there still remains the task of articulating the courage, energy, and readiness to make a move. Such factors cannot come from the negation of Babylon, but only from the positive valuing of Israel and its memory. Such positive factors will never be given by the empire, but will only be achieved by re-entering the memory, life, traditions, and self-understanding of this community.

In Isa. 54:1–4 the poet makes maximum use of the Sarah memory.[10] In 51:2–3, 2 Isaiah has already made appeal to the Sarah memory, but now that memory is fully embraced. The address is to the barren one. The whole early history of Israel is a history of barren women surprised by births. (Thus in addition to Sarah, also Rebekah [Gen.

25:21], Rachel [29:31], and Hannah [1 Sam. 1:2].) But Sarah is the model of barrenness (Gen. 11:30), the pivot point of all the memory. The motif of barrenness is a way Israel has of speaking of the future, the child of the next generation being given freely and graciously by God in spite of all circumstance. The future is always unmerited, unwarranted, and impossible for Israel. Yet it is given!

Verses 1–4 offer three sets of imperatives, each supported by a motivational clause introduced by "for" (*kî*). The form of *imperative* followed by *motivation* is the standard form of a hymn, as for example in Psalm 117.[11] The poem of Isaiah 54 then is an act of praise which in itself is a subversive act against the empire, for empires are not open to real doxology.

The first set of imperatives (v. 1a) is that the barren one should sing, the one who has never been in labor should cry in joy because her circumstance has changed. Any Israelite would know this refers to mother Sarah. The first motivational clause of v. 1 contrasts this desolate Sarah with the married one who is Babylon: "For the children of the desolate one will be more. . . ." That is the ground for the initial invitation to sing. The slave girl, not the imperial lady, is the one who has a future. The contrast looks back to the power of Israel when the midwives among the slaves were blessed with multiplication (Exod. 1). The tide of history has turned, so that the grand lady Babylon who has all the outer marks of power is shown to be irrelevant for the future. The future belongs to this desolate one who is surprised by the future.

The second set of imperatives is in v. 2. Five verbs are used: *enlarge, let stretch, hold back, lengthen,* and *strengthen.* The imperative here is not an allusion to the tradition but is quite concrete strategy inside the metaphor of many children. It is a happy worry that this family, newly blessed with many heirs, must firmly establish its tent. The place is going to be overrun with children so that the tent will collapse unless it is securely supported. The blessing of so many heirs—so much future—requires heavier tent pegs and stronger ropes. The poet here plays upon Israel's imagination to entertain an alternative scenario in which the future—so closed by Babylon—becomes flooded with possibility, crowded with new life and new hope.

The second motivational clause of v. 3 returns more directly to the Sarah-Abraham tradition. The references to "descendent," "possession," "the nations" are direct allusions which play upon the theme of Abraham as a father of many nations. It is a remarkably bold offer in the face of a situation in which Israel seems to be the servant of many nations. The poetry articulates the deep inversion and reversal which are necessary for life beyond the empire.

The third set of imperatives is in v. 4a, expressed in two parallel verbs: "do not fear," "do not be confounded." Perhaps this imperative is the crucial one theologically and rhetorically. "Do not fear" is standard form for a salvation oracle, much used by 2 Isaiah. It is regularly a response to a lament or complaint and is such a powerful authoritative intervention that it intends to "change the world."[12] The second imperative, "do not be confounded," perhaps comes much closer to the metaphor for barrenness. Barrenness in that ancient world was indeed a scandal, judged a curse from God. This speech announces the end of Sarah's season of humiliation, surely heard by exiles as an end to the season of political-cultural displacement and humiliation. The fear and humiliation are related to accepting life according to Babylonian definitions and perceptions. This promissory word of birth and hope breaks and nullifies all of the weighty, oppressive claims of the Babylonian empire.

The third set of motivation clauses are clear in v. 4:

> for you will not be ashamed,
> for you will not be put to shame.

The reason not to fear is that Yahweh has powerfully intervened. This text appears to be an intentional response to and refutation of the grief text of Jer. 31:15–19. Notice the grief of Jer. 31:16, the shame of v. 19.[13] In the poem of Jeremiah, Rachel grieves for the exiled children, Rachel is deeply ashamed and unable to be comforted. In that poem Rachel also functions as a reference for the grief and humiliation of exile. Our text (Isa. 54:1–4) with its appeal to Sarah intends to override the exilic grief of Rachel in Jer. 31:15–19. Together the two poems on Rachel and Sarah indicate the remarkable ways in which memory is mobilized to serve present pastoral issues.

The poem of Isaiah 54 thus far has three sets of imperatives, in vv. 1a, 2, 4, and three corresponding sets of motivations in vv. 1b, 3, 4. The hoped-for outcome of the poem is a new, fearless Israel no longer needing to accept a lesser spot assigned by the empire. Out of this memory, the poet reads energy, freedom, and self-identity into the life of Israel. People who have such poetry derived from their own memory are people exceedingly difficult to control or manipulate through the ways of conformity and despair. Such powerful memory maintains freedom of perception even in coercive situations.

The three sets of imperatives play upon the theme of barrenness and appeal to the memory of mother Sarah. The three sets of motivational clauses provide ground for hope because they promise that this same God who caused birth in the midst of barrenness is about to act again in transformative ways.

This opening part of the poem (vv. 1–4) is brought to a stunning climax in v. 4b (also an echo of Jer. 31:19), again introduced by "for":

> You will forget the shame. . . .
> The reproach . . . you will remember no more.

The poem is an act of remembering. But it is remembering in the present tense, for it is apparent to any contemporary of 2 Isaiah that the point to be scored is in the present imperial context. The memory functions to disclose the potential power of God's promise in the present. Under God's governance, the barrenness of Israel is to become more powerful then all the power of the imperial hegemony of Babylon.

In verses 5–10, the theme of new possibility is carried further through five statements (three of which begin with $k\hat{\imath}$). In a very general way, all five statements may be taken as further motivational clauses for the "fear not" of v. 4, but they are not closely linked to those imperatives.

Verse 5 is a general introduction to the metaphor of marriage: The creator is husband. Heretofore, Sarah had been seen as a mother. Now the metaphor is extended so that she is married to this creator who is identified in this verse in three traditional ways, as the warrior, as the redeemer of Israel, and as the God of all creation. Yahweh is indeed all of these agents but here all of the metaphors are singularly related to mother Sarah. The statement of v. 5 begins with a $k\hat{\imath}$. At the outset a motivational clause is given in which to ground hope.

The second motivational statement takes up the husband metaphor

in v. 6, again with *kî*. Here the old ancestral memory is turned precisely to make a possibility for exiles. The wife-Sarah-Israel is abandoned
(divorced) and, deeply grieved, cast off. This is the experience of
Israel in exile (cf. 49:14). Read theologically it could not be interpreted
in any other way. But the woman abandoned is called, acknowledged,
and reclaimed in relationship. Clearly if exile is abandonment by her
husband, then reclaiming the relation means the end of exile. The
point is not argued here vis-á-vis Babylonian power. Here it is asserted
only theologically in terms of God's powerful inclination. (See the
same themes used in parallel fashion in Isa. 62:4-5.)

The model of divorce-remarriage evolved in the poem out of the
earlier birth imagery and is explicated in vv. 6-8. The exile is acknowledged. It is real. It is caused by God. It is serious and painful. It happens because of overwhelming wrath. It did not happen for the reasons espoused by Babylon. We are not even given an argument that
Israel's sense of abandonment was justified. The poet is not interested
here in theodicy, but only in the metaphor leading to newness and
possibility.

But these verses do not dwell on exile that is for a brief moment.
The accent of these verses is on what is abidingly true and powerful in
the face of the exile. It is the reality of everlasting love (cf. Jer. 31:3),
which evokes the double use of the term compassion (vv. 7-8). The
ground for hope among exiles is Yahweh's everlasting love. The result
of that passionate commitment is, "I will gather" Israel and thereby
end exile. The announcement of that ending of exile concerns the compassion of God.[14] The exile has not disrupted God's passion for Israel.
God's compassion has been in abeyance, but not nullified. Now that
compassion which was momentarily dormant is again operative. Sarah-
Israel is the beloved spouse of Yahweh and is valued into the future.

In v. 9 the imagery shifts abruptly. The poet continues to play upon
the memory of Israel. We get a sense of the powerful freedom of the
poet rooted in the tradition, because the poet moves dramatically
from Abraham and Sarah to Noah. Who would have linked the two
traditions together as a way to reread exile! In appealing to the Noah
tradition, the poet makes a remarkable connection between flood and
exile. "This," meaning the exile, "is like the days of Noah." The exile
is experientially a parallel to the flood with its sense of disorder and

chaos. This poetry seems conventional to us, but what an extraordinary use of memory and what a brilliant imaginative act of intellect, to draw the parallel between flood and exile. The parallel permits the thought that the exile, like the flood, is due to wickedness. It also permits the linkage that in the exile, as in the flood, this treasured family of promise is provided a means of survival. But it is, in the third place, the resolution of both flood and exile that interests the poet. Exile is like the flood in a very particular way. Both are ended by the faithful promise of Yahweh (cf. Gen. 8:22; 9:8-17). In both acts, the promise of God is freely given, without cause or response on Israel's part. The promise in and of itself is world-changing. As the waters receded for Noah, so now the anger of Yahweh recedes, and as that happens, new possibility presents itself.

Verses 1-9 have been Israel's return to its memory, especially to Sarah, less centrally to Noah. Verse 10 represents a move from memory toward new possibility. It begins to state the implication and spin-off of the memory. The poem dares to assert that God's covenant loyalty is more reliable than the mountains and hills, that the covenant is more durable than creation. In Jer. 31:32-37 and 33:25-26 the argument is made that the covenant is as reliable as creation. Here the argument is escalated to say covenant is more reliable than creation. The promise of v. 10 seems to be an echo of the rainbow promise of Gen. 9:9-17, for it asserts that the covenant of peace will not be removed. The notion of a "covenant of peace" is also cited by Ezekiel 34:25, 37:26, texts nearly contemporaneous to our text. The phrase "will not be removed" is reminiscent of 2 Sam. 7:14-16, so that this perhaps also alludes to the Davidic promise (cf. Isa. 55:3). The climactic statement of v. 10 concerns God's compassion, reiterating the theme of vv. 7-8. Taken together, vv. 7-8, 10, buttressed as they are with reference to Noah, serve to deny that the exile is a rupture in God's commitment to Israel. Earlier Jeremiah and Ezekiel had stressed the discontinuity. Second Isaiah, by contrast, affirms that in the heart of God there was not a break in the history of compassion and fidelity.[15]

Re-entry into the memory requires and permits a rereading of the present reality. God is not absent. God is not defeated. God has not quit. God's powerful promises are still in effect. But the only way this can be asserted in the present is to reassert the whole history of promise that lies behind the present moment of the promise. It is our loss of historical perspective, our reduction of everything to the present moment that results in hopelessness. The promises of God have no credibility, to exiles or anyone else, unless they are seen over the generations. When the long-term, intergenerational power of the promises is forfeited, the present grows thin and hopeless. Options disappear, and dominant definitions of reality appear to be the only available ones. Thus, the practice of memory serves to open options in the reading of present reality. Memory prevents a reductionism that absolutizes current modes of domination. It leaves open the chance that new configurations are possible that arise out of the memory, configurations that are not excessively impressed by or committed to the present arrangement. When memory operates with such freedom as here, it leads to new historical possibility.

The new historical possibility of homecoming is firmly rooted in v. 10, which projects a season of compassion. The text makes a rhetorical and substantive turn between v. 10 and v. 11. Verses 1-10 reach back into memory. Verses 11-17 are a statement of new possibility derived from the memory. The address in v. 11 alludes back to Noah, "afflicted, storm tossed, not comforted." The entire memory of vv. 1-10 concerns invoking the comfort of God in the past as a ground for the present hope now to be announced.

The focus on the present in v. 11 is marked by "behold." What follows is the restoration of the city that Babylon had razed, with foundations, pinnacles, gates, walls (vv. 11b-12). The next generation will be comforted and blessed by prosperity (v. 13). There will be absence of oppression, fear, and terror (v. 14). Finally, vv. 15-17 announce the vindication of Israel, the powerful protection of city and people against every assault. This old poetry that moves from memory (vv. 1-10) to historical possibility (vv. 11-17) makes a striking connection between the two. As the shamed barren woman is given children, so the desolate abandoned city is given protection and well-being. The city destroyed by Babylon will not stay destroyed but is now guaranteed new well being, precisely and especially in the face of the empire. It is nothing o her than the memory that permits the poet to articulate new possibility, out beyond the empire.

AGAINST AMNESIA

This text is obviously addressed to exiles, to displaced Jews who are in Babylon.[16] We have only hints and traces of resistance to the poet, but we may imagine that the message of 2 Isaiah was not everywhere welcomed. Just as Jeremiah was taken as a traitor for encouraging submission to Babylon,[17] so the poet of 2 Isaiah must have been perceived, at least in some circles, as a traitor for proclaiming departure from the empire.

There are suggestions in the text that the Jewish community was either reluctant to follow the lead of 2 Isaiah or was doubtful of his credibility. The reluctance seems to be articulated in Isa. 45:9–13, in which the opponents of the poet seem to reject divine initiative, presumably with reference to naming an alien Cyrus Israel's liberator (messiah). The doubt of the community is likely reflected in 50:2, with a rhetorical question articulating an opinion among exiles: "Is my arm shortened?" That is, am I too weak to accomplish deliverance? The question and its vigorous answer mean to refute a doubting opinion in the community. Finally, in 49:14, the quotation attributed to Zion suggests that some felt Yahweh had abandoned Israel. These statements of doubt are probably derived from standard liturgies of lament.

Second Isaiah thus addressed his words against

those who refuse rescue by Cyrus (45:9–13)
those who doubt the power of God (50:2)
those who doubt the fidelity of God (49:14)

Who are these, then, to whom the text is an enemy? I suggest in the first instance, that the text means to refute those who suffer from amnesia, who have forgotten, disregarded, or jettisoned the tradition. They are those who may have neglected the tradition of liberation, of Sarah, of Noah. But they have forgotten because they have judged the old narrative affirmations to be irrelevant and without power. The enemies of this text are the ones who suffer from amnesia, who no longer tell the story or enquire about Yahweh (see Jer. 2:6–8). They may sense that Yahweh has forsaken them (Isa. 49:4), but in fact it is they who have forsaken Yahweh (see Jer. 2:13, 17, 19). Second Isaiah reiterates the memory with such insistence precisely because the memory has been judged to be nullified.

The result of amnesia most likely is that the Babylonian empire has come to be viewed as permanent, enduring, absolute, perpetual. These people have no memory of any other way. They can remember nothing except the present arrangement, which seems to have always been there.

If there is a lack of memory that can lead behind the present royal arrangement, it is likely also that there is an absence of openness to new historical possibility. The historical process is, without the critical function of memory, perceived as closed and settled. There is no leverage for any social change. There has always been a Babylonian empire and there must always be one. The opponents of 2 Isaiah cannot entertain the idea of a time in the future that will be different. We do not know if his addresses are resigned to Babylon in complacency or in resentment, but either way they seem resigned. They are without hope. People without historical sense and a proper practice of tradition are so bound in the "eternal now" that they finally end in despair.[18] This poem means to overcome the despair by assertion of new possibility yet to come.

THE REUSE OF ISRAEL'S MEMORY

In the New Testament, the function of memory to create historical possibility is a multifaceted issue. In important ways, the issue presents itself to us as a question of relating the Old Testament (as memory) to the gospel of Jesus (as a new possibility). This dynamic, as it operates between the testaments, is a very complicated matter. The New Testament in a variety of ways concerns continuity with the Old Testament, so that the memory of Israel functions as a positive force, and discontinuity from the Old Testament, so that the memory of Israel functions only as a foil.[19]

Here I pursue only one specific New Testament use of memory which evokes new possibility. The obvious choice is Galatians 3—4 in which Isa. 54:1 is quoted (Gal. 4:27). The problem that Paul seeks to address in Galatians is the relation of the gospel of free grace to the legal tradition of Judaism. In this particular letter Paul resists the insistence of the "Judaizers" that Christians must keep the Jewish law in order to be Christians. The odd form of Paul's argument is to juxtapose Hagar, who is Mt. Sinai, and Jerusalem, who is the mother of freedom. In Paul's presentation, the antitheses are never fully articulated in express parallelism, but the three sets of antitheses which may be interrelated are:

Isaac–Ishmael (who is not mentioned)
Sarah (not mentioned)–Hagar
Jerusalem–Sinai (Gal. 4:21–26).

The first set, Isaac-Sarah-Jerusalem, is the basis of freedom in the gospel. The second set, Ishmael-Hagar-Sinai, is the embodiment of legalism, that is, slavery.

In such a context, Isa. 54:1 is quoted. The barren one, again Sarah, is to have more children than the married one, presumably Hagar. The argument thus moves through two waves of memory, that of 2 Isaiah and of Abraham-Sarah. The allusion is directly to Isa. 54:1, so that Paul utilizes the exilic paradigm. But behind that is the Abraham-Sarah tradition in which the barren woman is given a son on no grounds other than the free promise of God.[20] Paul calls on the basic memory of the Old Testament that Israel's future is an act of free gift made against all expectations judged normal by the world.

The memory functions in Paul in a way quite parallel to its function in 2 Isaiah. What distinguished Paul from 2 Isaiah, of course, is the new historical possibility that is derived from memory. The new possibility for Paul is evangelical freedom, lived in a community based in promise that is not immobilized by oppressive obedience to the law. The memory is powerful, for the Babylonian figures of 2 Isaiah now speak to a different situation of despair and again evoke a fresh openness.

Thus the same memory can be turned in very different ways. Nonetheless, the historical possibility derived from the memory by 2 Isaiah and by Paul has important commonality. In both cases, the memory of this son given Sarah in the midst of barrenness serves to posit a new community not derived from or limited to the parameters of circumstance. Neither the force of the Babylonian empire, nor the force of Jewish law as Paul presents it, can nullify God's will for a community that trusts in God's promise.

This single promise out of the Abraham-Sarah tradition concerns God's unmerited newness. That promise is utilized in various ways in the gospel tradition. While the text regularly refers only to Abraham, the narrative base clearly depends on the centrality of Sarah. That the name of Sarah is missing in some of the allusions to the tradition may reflect a sexist tendency in flattening the memory. Thus, where the text reads "Abraham," it has no power without an intended reference to Sarah, the mother of Israel out of barrenness.

The Gospel of Luke makes dramatic use of the memory. In Luke 1:55 it is Mary who dares to trust in the inversion caused by new birth. In Luke 13:16 the woman with the infirmity, in the process of healing, is reckoned as a daughter of Abraham. In Luke 16:23-25, it is father Abraham who becomes the haven and refuge of the marginal one. In Luke 19:9, Zachaeus is reckoned as a son of Abraham. It is striking that in all four cases—Mary, the woman, Lazarus, and Zachaeus—the one who is peculiarly linked to Abraham (and Sarah) is the socially marginal one who alone seems to lack power for life.[21] It can be argued that the real source of newness is found in the reality of Jesus, rather than in the memory. But it remains a fact that the text has no way to mediate this newness except through the Abrahamic memory. Moreover, one has the impression that the references to Abraham are not casual or incidental but are carefully and intentionally stated. The Abrahamic references are not empty ciphers but are allusions to the power that can bring newness when none seemed possible. The narrative memory of Abraham and Sarah is thus offered as a source of vitality against a world that has been closed. Without Sarah and Abraham,

the song of Mary might never have envisioned an inversion,

the woman of infirmity might never have been redescribed in well-being,

the lot of Lazarus might not have been so reassuring,

and the future of Zachaeus might have not meshed so easily with the tradition.

In each case the memory functions to create a new social possibility, made possible by re-entry into this particular memory of barrenness and birth.

BABYLON AS CONTEMPORARY THREAT

It remains for us to ask about how Isa. 54:1-17 and the theme of memory allow possibility for our own situation. It is obvious that no simple analogy can be made, because the people with whom we minister are, on the whole, not materially displaced, not yearning for another place which we call home. Mostly we are people who are well-settled, who have an enormous stake in where we are. In one form or another, we are tenured there for the long haul.

But perhaps such a reading of our situation is too easy and misses the point. Indeed perhaps such a settled reading of reality is precisely the problem, because it is a reading of reality done without benefit of a text like Isa. 54:1–17. Perhaps it is the purpose of a text like this to require us to reread our situation in a very different way.

I suggest that reading our faith situation in light of such a text as this may put us in a new crisis, the very kind of crisis the text must have intended when it was first spoken to exiles. I propose three aspects of this text that bear upon our ministry:

1. *We incline to take Babylonian definitions of reality too much for granted.* That is what sixth-century Jews were inclined to do. As they found their way into this new culture, they forgot it was a strange land and came to regard it as home. They assimilated.

By analogy I suggest that Christians in our culture are greatly tempted to accept the definitions of reality that are given us by the dominant voices of our culture. This, of course, is not to say there are not good values in our culture, even as there were good values in a quite advanced Babylonian culture. The trouble comes, nonetheless, when those cultural modes are so much taken for granted that they are equated with the claims of faith. We may observe how very easily American Christianity comes to identify with Western capitalism, the free market system, and the values that grow from there. Or, more acutely, how easily we are enveloped into consumer militarism, which roughly characterizes the main value tendency of American society. Consumerism is the seduction that getting and having and using is the main mode of humanness. Militarism is an act of public power that defends and legitimates our inordinate privilege in the world. We live in that system long enough, we enjoy its benefits long enough, until we come to think of it as a given. There follows from these values certain hopes and expectations, certain fears and dreads. The whole package tends to be identified with the claims of Christian faith.

Not only does such a dominant system then come to appear normative and beyond fundamental criticism. It also seems ordained and authorized to be enduring, so that we cannot think apart from it, cannot remember a time without it, and cannot imagine a future time when life should be shaped differently. To take the dominant definitions of reality with such seriousness is to absolutize our present and to feel justified in defining it as the embodiment of God's will for us.

Such a temptation, I assume, is clear to us in terms of public policy, but it is equally the case in a more personal way. Consumer militarism (our particular form of Babylonian imperialism) not only shapes public policy but also goes far to shape personal identity and personal self-understanding. The values of consumerism as they are personally appropriated tend to an intense narcissism and an expectation of self-gratification. If one should ask basic questions as the catechism tradition asks,

> What should be man's chief concern? (*Westminster Catechism*)

or

> What is your only comfort and strength in this age and in the age to come? (*Heidelberg Catechism*)

the answer in our narcissism, when we answer honestly, is likely not to name God but to focus on self. My sense is that in the context of faith in American Christianity, precisely such a situation has been accepted wherein the dominant values of the imperial system have become the normative prism for our faith. Babylon seems to be of overriding importance and authority even today.

2. *The counter theme is that the old peculiar memories of the faith community have been lost, forgotten, muted, or distorted.* The community suffers from amnesia. The Jews in Babylon, we may suspect, were not overwhelmingly preoccupied with the separatist tradition. They likely were busy getting along and making their way in this foreign culture. As a result, the old narrative memory became a luxury for special nostalgic occasions or the practice of irrelevant fanatics. Disregard of the memory is the price of embracing a different way in the world.

The extent to which this is true by analogy in our situation needs yet to be determined. It is my impression that this exactly what has happened in American Christianity. The American value system is of such overriding and visible force among us that the story of this community of faith seems only marginally important. Where it is recited and remembered, it is done in ways that concede the main points to the imperial story.[22]

This surely is the case with liberal Christianity. Indeed the peculiar memory is something of an embarrassment. We are inclined to want the ethical and political spinoffs of the memory, but without the concrete particularity of the memory itself. As a result, liberals incline to sound mostly like social scientists who have lost confidence in the memory and who have reached a value commitment on quite alien grounds.

But the conservative backlash in the church tends to be no more honorable. For all the pious sounds of conservative urgency, this religion also does not permit itself to be illuminated by the core tradition.[23] Rather, it picks and chooses a few items and presents an agenda that echoes the forces of reactionism about security and sexuality. But it also does not show us how to listen to and be addressed by the narrative memory. This distorted handling of tradition serves simply to reinforce the voices of stability and control in the empire.

The purpose of the memory has regularly been to provide critical standing ground for imagination that has not been co-opted. The memory of Sarah, as we have it in our text, is to remind us that the future is not limited to imperial definitions of reality and possibility, because there is at work this other one who strangely does impossible things on our behalf. The memory of the Noah tradition, as we have it in our text, is to affirm to us that experience of chaos (flood), real as it is, is not the ultimate word, because there is one who presides over the chaos. Therefore, we need not take upon ourselves the dread task of managing all forms of chaos, attempting to impose our order, which can finally never displace the sure order of God.

The function of the Sarah and Noah memories is to impinge upon present definitions of reality and to keep them open and provisional. They remind us of another time when life was given and guarded without Babylonian defenses. They attest to us that the one who worked in these stories out of compassion and loyalty is the one still at work in our story. We are thereby permitted to contemplate futures that are not Babylonian, but that give us freedom and possibility for an alternative ordering of social life.

The memory gives us freedom, flexibility, and distance in relation to present definitions of reality and arrangement of power. Where the memory is muted or distorted, we will, unlike Sarah, trust only obvious possibilities. We will, unlike Noah, come to believe that the present guards against chaos are the only ones available. When the memory is forgotten, we will come to trust excessively in Babylonian modes of life as the only thinkable, possible modes. We will become docile, passive, submissive subjects of the empire, glad to have our life-world contained in the imperial system which is the solution. Where memory is lost or nullified, we are left with only a narrow range of present-tense systems to which excessive commitment is often made.

3. The combination of taking Babylonian definitions of reality too seriously and the loss of the peculiar memories of the faith community leads to one life-destroying result: *despair*. On the one hand, present arrangements of power seem absolute. On the other hand, the critical capacity to imagine the world organized differently is forfeited with the loss of memory. The only conclusion to draw is that the way the world is, is the way it will always be. Such a condition for being hopeless can, of course, be a destructive, depressing condition. Or conversely, such absolutizing of the present can be a mistakenly felt good, which imagines that the happy present is eternally guaranteed. Either way life is set into present configurations of poverty and wealth, of misery and well-being. Neither the rich in their complacency nor the poor in their despair imagine that the world could be different. For those who yearn for the world to be different, but dare not hope, the outcome may be destructive self-hatred or destructive violence. On the other hand, those who desire the world to be always the way it presently is may defend it because the present configuration is regarded as proper, legitimate, and beneficial. The two parties of despair serve each other, the one bent on destructiveness, the other committed to repression and defense at any cost.

I suspect that it was the same way for Jews in Babylon. The voice of the empire seems forever (cf. Isaiah 47). The subservient Jews accepted it so. In that situation 2 Isaiah's appeal to memories of impossibility was powerfully subversive because it dared open options and practice criticism. It put the claim of the empire into a broader context where it was shown not to be absolute. It bore witness to another agent on whom the empire did not reckon.

I submit that the same situation of *imperialism, amnesia,* and *despair* is powerful among us. Only memory can give a sense of possibility against the empire. Mother Sarah stands over this community of faith as a concrete sign that dominant definitions of reality do not always prevail.

In comparing white and black writers, Alice Walker observes:

> for the most part, white American writers tended to end their books and their characters' lives as if there were no better existence for which to struggle. The gloom of defeat is thick. By comparison, black writers seem always involved in a moral and/or physical struggle, the result of which is expected to be some kind of larger freedom. Perhaps this is because our literary tradition is based on the slaves' narratives, where escape for the body and freedom for the soul went together. Or perhaps this is because black people have never felt themselves guilty of global cosmic sin. [24]

The ideology of the empire thrives on global, cosmic sin. Second Isaiah, like black literature, is based on slave narratives from Exodus. It invites to "some kind of larger freedom." Such larger freedom is a possibility for exiles, but only where the slave narratives are re-entered and claimed as ours—even in a foreign land.

The poet in exile sings his people to homecoming. And that is a theme to which the exiled church in America is now summoned. The gospel is that we may go home. Home is not here in the consumer militarism of a dominant value system. Home also is not in heaven, as though we may escape. Home, rather, is God's kingdom of love and justice and peace and freedom that waits for us. The news is we are invited home (cf. Luke 15:17). The whole church may yet sing: "Precious Saviour take my hand. Lead me home!"

CONCLUSION:
HURT AS HOPE'S HOME

THE METAPHOR SUGGESTED in all the literature of Jeremiah, Ezekiel, 2 Isaiah is exile. It is proposed that these literary-theological traditions of exile and homecoming offer a poignant way to read our cultural-religious situation and to lead us to hopeful imagination. Serious believers are indeed an alien community in American culture.[1] In considering these three prophetic-poetic traditions, I have thematized as follows:

1. From Jeremiah: The grief of Jeremiah and of God permit newness, for newness comes out of grief articulated and embraced.
2. From Ezekiel: The holiness of God becomes the ground for serious hope, for no hope will be found as long as it is reduced to things useful, short of God's holiness.
3. From 2 Isaiah: The practice of memory permits articulation of new possibilities, for memory is the only alternative to absolutizing imperial claims.

In such a thematization I suggest that the literature means to engage and speak against a major cultural temptation:

1. *Grief* is offered against establishment *denial* and *cover-up* that Jeremiah regards as a lie.
2. *Holiness* is proclaimed against conventional theology that never quite faces the otherness and always hopes for and forms a *utilitarianism* that links God's holiness to some historical purpose.
3. *Memory* is asserted against *amnesia* in which nothing is noticed or

critiqued and everything is absolutized in its present form.

Thus, I take *denial, utilitarianism,* and *amnesia* to be the context in which the gospel is now to be proclaimed and practiced.

It will be clear in making this threefold argument that I have in fact made the same argument three times in different modes:

1. *Grief* should permit newness.
2. *Holiness* should give hope.
3. *Memory* should allow possibility.

All three affirmations argue that life comes out of death. Thus, in three ways I mean to affirm that the structure of theological argument is congenial to an evangelical theology of the cross,[2] though of course I have not done so in any christological way. The experience of Israel is about brokenness and surprise, which comes to be the shape of the Jesus story. Indeed, the New Testament portrayal of Jesus is surely the rereading of the experience of Israel.

Insofar as my analysis touches our situation, I propose that the texts of Jeremiah, Ezekiel, and 2 Isaiah are a main resource for serious Christians who find themselves in an alienated cultural situation, a resource for hopeful imagination today. If this is a fair statement of the structure of biblical faith, then serious believers must see that this faith contradicts dominant cultural perspectives that *deny grief, co-opt holiness,* and *nullify memory* in the interest of an absolute present.

Finally, I have prefixed each of these formulas by "only." It will need to be tested to see whether this claims too much. I think not. I understand this "only" to be theologically resonant with the "only" that Luther discerned in Rom. 3:28. Luther in his exposition of "grace alone, Christ alone, Scripture alone" went beyond the actual words of the text to assert its radical evangelical claim. In the same way the "only" is not explicit in our texts but surely is implicit. It is precisely the "only" that is at stake for exiled, alienated Christians against imperial ideology. If the "only" does not hold, then there is no point to be made by this argument.

1. If newness can come elsewhere than out of grief, then grief does not fully matter. But we have argued out of Jeremiah that it is *only grief* that permits newness—nothing else.
2. If hope can come from elsewhere than God's holiness, then

God's holiness is not finally important. But we have argued that it is *only holiness* that gives hope—nothing else.

3. If possibility can come from other than memory, then memory need not finally be bothered with. But we have argued that it is *only memory* that allows possibility—nothing else.

But if the "only" holds, as I believe it surely does, then the children and heirs of these texts know something decisive and have something crucial entrusted to them. What is known and trusted is enough to restore vitality to ministry if we have the courage to think through, see through, and act through the mystery of which we are stewards.

NOTES

INTRODUCTION

1. On the commonality of these traditions, see Gerhard von Rad, *Old Testament Theology* (New York: Harper & Row, 1965), 2:263–77; and Thomas R. Raitt, *A Theology of Exile* (Philadelphia: Fortress Press, 1977).

2. For a general introduction to the literary-theological traditions set in the exile, see Ralph W. Klein, *Israel in Exile* (Philadelphia: Fortress Press, 1979); and Peter Ackroyd, *Exile and Restoration* (Philadelphia: Westminster Press, 1968).

3. Thus the hinge between *Old Testament Theology I* (New York: Harper & Row, 1962) and *Old Testament Theology II* is stated as this passage in the frontispiece of the second volume. By such an arrangement, von Rad sought to express both the continuity and the discontinuity that belong to the juxtaposition of tradition and prophecy.

4. But see the important statement of discontinuity by Walther Zimmerli, "Prophetic Proclamation and Reinterpretation," in *Tradition and Theology in Old Testament,* ed. D. A. Knight (Philadelphia: Fortress Press, 1977), 69–100.

5. It is important to note the suggestive interpretation of "new things" in 2 Isaiah given by Brevard Childs, *Introduction to the Old Testament as Scripture* (Philadelphia: Fortress Press, 1979), 325–30; and Ronald E. Clements, "The Unity of the Book of Isaiah," *Interpretation* 36 (1982): 117–29.

6. On the ways in which language creates worlds, see Amos N. Wilder, "Story and Story-World," *Interpretation* 37 (1983): 353–64. The sociological dimensions of this power of language are made clear by Peter Berger and Thomas Luckmann, *The Social Construction of Reality* (Garden City, N.Y.: Doubleday & Co., 1966).

7. On this thematization, see Ronald E. Clements, "Patterns in the Prophetic Canon," in *Canon and Authority,* ed. G. W. Coats and B. O. Long

(Philadelphia: Fortress Press, 1977), 42–55.

8. For a remarkable example of the way in which the text was loosened from its historical rootage and interpreted through contemporary experience, see the comments on Ibn Ezra's interpretation of exilic Isaiah by U. Simon, "Ibn Ezra between Medievalism and Modernism: The Case of Isaiah x–xvi," *Vetus Testamentum,* Supplements 36 (1985): 257–71.

9. In what follows I will refer to all three traditions, including Ezekiel, as "poets." On Ezekiel as poet, see Amos Wider, *Theopoetic* (Philadelphia: Fortress Press, 1976), 101–2.

10. On relinquishment, see Marie Augustus Neal, *A Socio-Theology of Letting Go* (New York: Paulist Press, 1977). As Neal understands, the required relinquishment is not only economic but includes every dimension of life, spiritual, emotional, social.

11. See Langdon Gilkey, *Society and the Sacred* (New York: Crossroad, 1981). See also Michael Harrington, *The Politics of God's Funeral* (New York: Holt, Rinehart & Winston, 1983).

12. In large scope I am using for interpretation what James A. Sanders has called "dynamic analogy" (*God Has a Story Too* [Philadelphia: Fortress Press, 1979], esp. 20).

13. Charles Gerkin, who stresses "interpretation" as a key to pastoral care, points in a most helpful direction (*The Living Human Document* [Nashville: Abingdon Press, 1984]).

CHAPTER 1

1. James Crenshaw, "A Living Tradition," *Interpretation* 37 (1983): 117–29, has reviewed the issues and the alternative solutions now offered. See also *Prophet to the Nations, Essays in Jeremiah Studies,* ed. L. G. Perdue and B. W. Kovacs (Winona Lake, Ind.: Eisenbrauns, 1984).

2. Ernest W. Nicholson, *Preaching to the Exiles* (Oxford: Blackwell, 1970), has proposed that the book of Jeremiah has been heavily reworked in order to be pertinent to the theological crisis of the exile, so that the book reflects the creative work of that generation. In this he is largely followed by Eberhard von Waldow in his forthcoming work in The Forms of the Old Testament Literature project. See also Robert P. Carroll, *From Chaos to Covenant* (New York: Crossroad, 1981).

3. See now also Peter R. Ackroyd, "The Book of Jeremiah—Some Recent Studies," *Journal for the Study of the Old Testament* 28 (1984): 47–59.

4. John Bright, *Jeremiah,* Anchor Bible (Garden City, N.Y.: Doubleday & Co., 1965).

5. See the preliminary statement of William Holladay, *Jeremiah: Spokesman Out of Time* (Philadelphia: United Church Press, 1974). His major commentary is in the Hermeneia series: *Jeremiah,* vol. 1 (Philadelphia:

Fortress Press, 1986). See his provisional construction of a chronology, "The Years of Jeremiah's Preaching," *Interpretation* 37 (1983): 146–59.

6. Brevard S. Childs, *Introduction*, 345–54.

7. On this pervasive juxtaposition in the prophets, see Ronald E. Clements, "Patterns in the Prophetic Canon," *Canon and Authority*, ed. by G. W. Coats and B. O. Long (Philadelphia: Fortress Press, 1977), 42–55.

8. See Walter Brueggemann, "The Book of Jeremiah; Portrait of the Prophet," *Interpretation* 37 (1983): 130–45, for a characterization that makes no claim concerning historical matters.

9. A decision to include vv. 15–18 in the call portrayal would indicate that the call may be retrospective, i.e., fully aware of the opposition to be encountered. This is consistent with the same matter in Ezekiel and Isaiah, on which see Carroll, *Chaos*, chap. 2.

10. Notice that in this translation, "against" reflects two different Hebrew prepositions, first *'al* and then *le*.

11. On the significance of this dismantling of the temple apparatus, one must be clear on the crucial importance of the temple for the life of the community. See John M. Lundquist, "What is a Temple: A Preliminary Typology," in *The Quest for the Kingdom of God*, ed. by H. B. Huffmon, et al. (Winona Lake, Ind.: Eisenbrauns, 1983), 205–19.

12. Norman Habel, "The Form and Significance of the Call Narrative," *Zeitschrift für die alttestamentliche Wissenschaft* 77 (1965): 297–323.

13. H. Graf Reventlow, *Liturgie und prophetisches Ich bei Jeremia* (Gutersloh: Gerd Mohn, 1963), 24–77.

14. Childs, *Introduction*, 347–50.

15. Thus both Babylon and Jeremiah are characterized according to the metaphor of unbreakable metal. That both are characterized in the same way suggests that the prophet and the empire are allied against Jerusalem.

16. On prayer as combat, see Jacques Ellul, *Prayer and Modern Man* (New York: Seabury Press, 1970), chap. 5. Worth noting in this connection is Rom. 15:30 in which Paul speaks of prayer as combat. Paul's discernment of this, as of so many things, is most congenial to the tradition of Jeremiah.

17. On the confessions, see Gerhard von Rad, "The Confessions of Jeremiah," in *Theodicy in the Old Testament*, ed. by J. L. Crenshaw (Philadelphia: Fortress Press, 1983), 88–99; and John Bright, "Jeremiah's Complaints—Liturgy or Expressions of Personal Distress?" in *Proclamation and Presence*, ed. by J. I. Durham and J. R. Porter (London: SCM Press, 1970), 189–214.

18. On this aspect of Jeremiah, see the poignant statement of Elie Wiesel, *Five Biblical Portraits* (Notre Dame: Univ. of Notre Dame Press, 1981), 97–127.

19. On metaphors of hurt and healing in Jeremiah, see James Muilenburg, "The Terminology of Adversity in Jeremiah," in *Translating and Under-*

standing the Old Testament, ed. by H. T. Frank and W. L. Reed (New York: Abingdon Press, 1970), 42-63.

20. Juan Luis Segundo, *The Hidden Motives of Pastoral Action* (Maryknoll, N.Y.: Orbis Books, 1978), identifies the hidden motive as fear that the faith claim is not true.

21. Langdon Gilkey, *Society.* See also Michael Harrington, *Politics.*

22. The fact of the call is subordinate to the substance of the commission. J. Christian Beker, *Paul the Apostle: The Triumph of God in Life and Thought* (Philadelphia: Fortress Press, 1980), has helpfully made the same judgment concerning Paul.

23. See the sociological analysis of Daniel Yankelovitch, *New Rules* (New York: Random House, 1981).

24. See James W. Fowler, *Becoming Adult, Becoming Christian* (San Francisco: Harper & Row, 1984).

25. See Christopher Lasch, *The Culture of Narcissism* (New York: Norton, 1979). See also Robert Bellah et al., *Habits of the Heart* (Berkeley and Los Angeles: Univ. of California Press, 1985); and Alasdair MacIntyre, *After Virtue* (Notre Dame: Univ. of Notre Dame Press, 1981).

26. See Brueggemann, *The Creative Word* (Philadelphia: Fortress Press, 1982), chap. 3.

27. On this confrontation, see Henri Mottu, "Jeremiah vs. Hananiah: Ideology and Truth in Old Testament Prophecy," in *The Bible and Liberation,* ed. by N. K. Gottwald (Maryknoll, N.Y.: Orbis Books, 1983), 235-51; and Hans Walter Wolff, *Confrontations with Prophets* (Philadelphia: Fortress Press, 1983), 63-76.

28. See esp. the question posed in Job 21:7, and Brueggemann, "Theodicy in a Social Dimension," *Journal for the Study of the Old Testament* 33 (1985): 3-25.

29. On the juxtaposition of spirituality and theodicy, see Brueggemann, *The Messages of the Psalms* (Minneapolis: Augsburg Pub. House, 1984), 168-76.

30. See the programmatic statement of Juan Luis Segundo, *The Community Called Church; A Theology for Artisans of a New Humanity* (Maryknoll, N.Y.: Orbis Books, 1973). The poetic quality of the prophetic becomes crucial when it is recognized that they work primarily against ideology. They seek to "disclose" what is "closed." George Anastaplo, *The Artist as Thinker* (Columbus: Ohio Univ. Press, 1983), 11, writes, "those whom the ancient Israelites called 'prophets,' the equally ancient Greeks call 'poets.'"

31. On the cruciality of the visioning process, see Craig Dykstra, *Vision and Character* (New York: Paulist Press, 1981). The work of Stanley Hauerwas is related to this understanding of personality theory.

32. On the power of metaphor for the forming of the world, see Sallie McFague, *Metaphorical Theology* (Philadelphia: Fortress Press, 1982). Frederick Herzog, "Liberation and Imagination," *Interpretation* 32 (1978):

227–41, has well understood the relation between such linguistic imagination and the reality of social freedom.

33. On the capacity of imaginative narrative to present alternative worlds, see Amos N. Wilder, "Story."

34. Paul Ricoeur, *The Philosophy of Paul Ricoeur,* ed. C. E. Reagan and D. Stewart (Boston: Beacon Press, 1979), esp. chaps. 15 and 16.

35. On the battle for imagination, see Amos Wilder, *Jesus' Parables and the War of Myths: Essays on Imagination in the Scripture* (Philadelphia: Fortress Press, 1983).

36. See Brueggemann, *David's Truth in Israel's Imagination and Memory* (Philadelphia: Fortress Press, 1985).

37. The account of the burning of the scroll in Jer. 36 is an early model of "book burning" as an effort to control and stifle subversive imagination.

38. See John Dominic Crossan, *The Dark Interval* (Allen, Tex.: Argus Communications, 1975); and Wilder's *Jesus' Parables.*

39. See Brueggemann, "'Impossibility' and Epistemology in the Faith Tradition of Abraham and Sarah (Gen. 18:1–15)," *Zeitschrift für die alttestamentliche Wissenschaft* 94 (1982): 614–34.

40. On the danger of poets, see the shrewd judgment of Miguel de Cervantes, *Don Quixote* (New York: Modern Library, 1950), 36: "What would be worse yet, turn poet, which they say is a catching and an incurable disease."

41. See Thomas W. Overholt, *The Threat of Falsehood: A Study in the Theology of the Book of Jeremiah* (London: SCM Press, 1970).

42. On the newness, see Wolff, *Confrontations,* 49–62; and the anguished statement of Emil Fackenheim, "New Hearts and the Old Covenant: On Some Possibilities of a Fraternal Jewish-Christian Reading of the Jewish Bible Today," in *The Divine Helmsman,* ed. J. L. Crenshaw and S. Sandmel (New York: Ktav, 1980), 191–205.

CHAPTER 2

1. On the centrality of grief and pathos in the tradition of Jeremiah, see Abraham Heschel, *The Prophets* (New York: Harper & Row, 1962), chap. 6, and more generally chaps. 12—15; Kazo Kitamori, *Theology of the Pain of God* (Richmond: John Knox Press, 1965); and most recently Terence Fretheim, *The Suffering of God* (Philadelphia: Fortress Press, 1984). See the helpful discussion of Kenneth R. Mitchell and Herbert Anderson, *All Our Losses, All Our Griefs* (Philadelphia: Westminster Press, 1983).

2. Granger Westberg, *Good Grief* (Philadelphia: Fortress Press, 1962).

3. Elizabeth Kubler-Ross, *On Death and Dying* (New York: Macmillan, 1969).

4. On the end of the system, see Robert J. Lifton, *The Broken Connection* (New York: Simon and Schuster, 1980). Lifton sees the connection between

the end of the symbol system and the end of social, political, economic systems.

5. For a critical analysis of this text, see Walter Brueggemann, "The 'Uncared' Now Cared For (Jer. 30:12-17): A Methodological Consideration," *Journal of Biblical Literature* 104 (1985): 419-28.

6. See the radical and influential statement of Robert Carroll, *Chaos.*

7. On Jeremiah's use of fresh and powerful metaphors, see esp. James Muilenburg, "The Terminology of Adversity in Jeremiah," in *Translating and Understanding the Old Testament,* 42-63. On the theological function of metaphors, see more programmatically Sallie McFague, *Metaphorical Theology.*

8. Patrick D. Miller, Jr., *Sin and Judgment in the Prophets* (Chico, Calif.: Scholars Press, 1982), has explored the close correspondence of sin and punishment. See his comments on our passage on p. 69.

9. On the power of words to form worlds, see Amos Wilder, "Story." See more broadly *Jesus' Parables,* also by Wilder.

10. On the historical and theological force of the destruction of 587 as a complete break point, see Walther Zimmerli, *I Am Yahweh* (Atlanta: John Knox Press, 1982), 111-33. Zimmerli speaks of "point zero."

11. On the transformation of God's heart, see my exposition of the flood narrative in *Genesis* (Atlanta: John Knox Press, 1982), 73-88; idem, "A Shape for Old Testament Theology (II: Embrace of Pain)," *Catholic Biblical Quarterly* 47 (1985): 395-415.

12. See the discerning exposition of the Beatitudes as they are related to social reality by Michael Crosby, *The Spirituality of the Beatitudes* (Maryknoll, N.Y.: Orbis Books, 1981).

13. On the cruciality of grief as a social practice, see Brueggemann, "A Cosmic Sign of Relinquishment," *Currents in Theology and Mission* 11 (1984): 5-20.

14. See the analysis of Morris Silver, *Prophets and Markets* (Boston: Kluwer Nijhoff Publishers, 1983), 225, 227 n. 25. Silver refers to Jeremiah as a "quisling." My impression is that Silver has all the facts right but fails to understand what is at issue in the text.

15. On the odd juxtaposition of two postmodern religious phenomena, see Harvey Cox, *Religion in the Secular City: Toward a Postmodern Theology* (New York: Simon & Schuster, 1984).

CHAPTER 3

1. See Robert McAfee Brown, *Elie Wiesel, Messenger to All Humanity* (Notre Dame: Univ. of Notre Dame Press, 1983), 154. The rabbis in the story are all "erudite and pious men."

2. See Claus Westermann, "The Role of the Lament in the Theology of the

Old Testament,'' in *Praise and Lament in the Psalms* (Atlanta: John Knox Press, 1981), 259–80.

3. On the cruciality of the priestly role in relation to "defilement," see Paul Ricoeur, *The Symbolism of Evil* (New York: Harper & Row, 1967). For a critical sense of religious impurity, see Fernando Belo, *A Materialist Reading of Mark* (Maryknoll, N.Y.: Orbis Books, 1981).

4. For critical background to the Ezekiel tradition, see the two important commentaries by Walter Zimmerli, *Ezekiel,* vol. 1, Hermeneia (Philadelphia: Fortress Press, 1979); *Ezekiel,* vol. 2, Hermeneia (Philadelphia: Fortress Press, 1983); and Moshe Greenberg, *Ezekiel 1—20,* Anchor Bible (Garden City, N.Y.: Doubleday & Co., 1983). See also the splendid issue of *Interpretation* (38/2 [1984]).

5. On the canonical shape of the Ezekiel tradition, see Brevard S. Childs, *Introduction,* 360–72.

6. I will disregard the oracles against the nations in chaps. 25—32, on which see Childs, *Introduction,* 366–67.

7. Abraham Heschel, *Who is Man?* (Stanford: Stanford Univ. Press, 1965), has eloquently protested against the reduction of human life, so that everything and everyone is a commodity to be used.

8. There is no doubt that the classic study of Rudolf Otto, *The Idea of the Holy* (New York: Oxford Univ. Press, 1923), is important and insightful. But it does not fully articulate the juxtaposition of threat and morality that belongs to Israel's discernment of God.

9. On this chapter, see Georg Fohrer, "The Righteous Man in Job 31," in *Essays in Old Testament Ethics,* ed. James L. Crenshaw and John T. Willis (New York: Ktav, 1974), 1–22; and the basic study of K. Galling, "Der Beichtspiegel," *Zeitschrift für die alttestamentliche Wissenschaft* 47 (1929): 125–30.

10. See Pablo Richard, ed., *The Idols of Death and the God of Life* (Maryknoll, N.Y.: Orbis Books, 1983).

11. On the claims of the Zion tradition and especially Ezekiel's investment in those claims, see Jon D. Levenson, *Sinai and Zion* (New York: Winston Press, 1985), esp. 115–16.

12. On these chapters see the analysis of Michael Fishbane, "Sin and Judgment in the Prophecies of Ezekiel," *Interpretation* 38 (1984): 137–50.

13. See von Rad, "The Form-Critical Problem of the Hexateuch," *The Problem of the Hexateuch and Other Essays* (1966; reprint Eng. trans., London: SCM Press, 1984).

14. See, e.g., Barbara Brown Zikmund, ed., *Hidden Histories of the United Church of Christ* (New York: United Church of Christ Press, 1984).

15. For a consideration of "history-makers" from below and "history-stoppers" from above, see Walter Brueggemann, "Blessed are the History-Makers," in *Hope Within History* (forthcoming, John Knox Press).

16. This passage and role in the tradition of Ezekiel has been definitely studied by H. Graf Reventlow, *Wachter über Israel. Ezechiel und seine Tradition,* Beihefte zur *ZAW* 1962 (Berlin: Töpelmann, 1962).

17. The problem of the dumbness of Ezekiel is exceedingly difficult. See Greenberg, *Ezekiel 1—20,* 79, for a review of the problem. See also Greenberg, "On Ezekiel's Dumbness," *Journal of Biblical Literature* 77 (1958): 101-5; and R. R. Wilson, "An Interpretation of Ezekiel's Dumbness," *Vetus Testamentum* 22 (1972): 91-104.

18. See the eloquent discussion of the issue by Andre Neher, *The Exile of the Word* (Philadelphia: Jewish Publication Society of America, 1981).

19. On these chapters, see Werner E. Lemke, "Life in the Present and Hope for the Future," *Interpretation* 38 (1984): 165-80; and Moshe Greenberg, "The Design and Themes of Ezekiel's Program of Restoration," *Interpretation* 38 (1984): 181-208. On chapters 40—48, see Jon Levenson, *Theology of the Program of Restoration of Ezekiel 40—48* (Missoula, Mont.: Scholars Press, 1976); and more critically, Paul D. Hanson, *The Dawn of Apocalyptic* (Philadelphia: Fortress Press, 1975), chap. 3.

20. Arguing from Micah 2:1-5, Albrecht Alt has shown that there is a persistent hope in Israel that the land will be redistributed. On the sociology of such a vision of land, see Frank Anthony Spina, "Israelites as *gerim,* 'Sojourners,' in Social and Historical Context," in *The Word of the Lord Shall Go Forth,* ed. C. L. Meyers and M. O'Connor (Winona Lake, Ind.: Eisenbrauns, 1983), 321-35. More broadly, see Norman K. Gottwald, *The Tribes of Yahweh* (Maryknoll, N.Y.: Orbis Books, 1979).

21. Too much should not be made of it, but it is telling that in Ezek. 8:6 it is Yahweh who is made a displaced, landless person. Most of the exilic theology has Yahweh making Israel an exile, but in this text, the process is inverted so that Yahweh is the one who is deported from the land.

22. Walther Zimmerli, "Plans for Rebuilding after the Catastrophe of 587," in *I Am Yahweh,* 111-33, has used the term "null point" with reference to this historical, theological crisis.

CHAPTER 4

1. On the context and literary shape of Ezekiel, see Peter Ackroyd, *Exile and Restoration* (Philadelphia: Westminster Press, 1968); Ralph W. Klein, *Israel in Exile* (Philadelphia: Fortress Press, 1979), 69-96; and Brevard S. Childs, *Introduction,* 339-54.

2. On the fundamental symbolic power of defilement and uncleanness, see Paul Ricoeur, *Symbolism.*

3. See Samuel Terrien, *The Elusive Presence* (New York: Harper & Row, 1979), on the text and issues related to the problem of presence.

4. For the normative explication of this and related formulae, see Walther

Zimmerli, *I Am Yahweh,* 1–110.

5. See the analysis of von Rad, "'Righteous' and 'Life' in the Cultic Language of the Psalms," *The Problem of the Hexateuch and Other Essays* (New York: McGraw-Hill, 1966), 243–66. See the comments on Ezekiel 18, in chap. 3 of this book.

6. See John Dillenberger, *God Hidden and Revealed* (Philadelphia: Muhlenburg Press, 1953), for a programmatic statement. For a recent study of the theme in the Psalms, see Samuel E. Ballentine, *The Hidden God: The Hiding of the Face of God in the Old Testament* (New York: Oxford Univ. Press, 1983).

7. On these chapters of new possibility, see Werner E. Lemke, "Life in the Present and Hope for the Future," *Interpretation* 38 (1984): 165–80.

8. I exclude from consideration here chap. 35, because it concerns Yahweh's sovereignty over the nations and only indirectly touches our theme.

9. A. Vanlier Hunter, *Seek the Lord* (Baltimore, Md.: St. Mary's Press, 1982), has argued that the prophets characteristically do not expect repentance or a change of heart but conclude that the time for such change has already passed.

10. The language here seems reminiscent of Hos. 2:23–25. The juxtaposition of renewal of creation and renewal of covenant is important for prophetic hope. On the links between the two, see Walter Harrelson, *From Fertility Cult to Worship* (Garden City, N.Y.: Doubleday & Co., 1969).

11. Paul Tournier, *The Strong and the Weak* (Philadelphia: Westminster Press, 1963), 13–19, has a discerning analysis of just such a situation and the power dynamics that operate.

12. See Zimmerli, *I Am Yahweh,* 111, 115, 133. See my concluding comments in chap. 3.

13. Amos Wilder, "A Hard Death," *Poetry* 107 (1965–66): 168–69, has a telling poetic line concerning such a historical context: "The zero hour breeds new algebras." The verb "breeds" seems to me to be just right, for how else might one speak of the strange surprise of newness?

14. On this difficult problem of the presence of David materials in Ezek. 34: 22–23 and 37:21–28, see Jon D. Levenson, *Theology of the Program of Restoration* (Missoula, Mont.: Scholars Press, 1976), esp. chap. 2—"Kingship and Theocracy in the Exile."

15. On the theme of inutility, see the discussion of Jacques Ellul, "Meditation on Utility," in *The Politics of God and the Politics of Man* (Grand Rapids: Wm. B. Eerdmans, 1972), 190–99.

16. On making use of God instrumentally, see Juan Luis Segundo, *The Hidden Motives.*

17. After I had completed the connection made here between Ezekiel and this parable, I discovered a helpful and supportive comment by Edward Schweizer, *The Good News According to Luke* (Atlanta: John Knox Press, 1984), 283. He writes of the Pharisee in this parable: "He is no longer willing

to let God be God but remains trapped in a world where persons seek recognition without God." This comment corresponds precisely to my reading of Ezekiel.

18. On this prayer, see my analysis in *David's Truth*.

19. For a recent appeal to Schleiermacher, see Peter Berger, *The Heretical Imperative* (Garden City, N.Y.: Anchor Books, 1979).

20. For a discerning and harsh critique of Maslow and the psychology of self-fulfillment, see Daniel Yankelovich, *New Rules,* 234–43. See the analysis of this social pathology by Robert Bellah et al., *Habits of the Heart*.

21. That the biblical God is not neutral is, of course, well established in the hermeneutics of liberation theology. Special reference should be made to the assertion of the Medellin Conference which spoke of "God's preferential option for the poor." On this, see Gustavo Gutierrez, *The Power of the Poor in History* (Maryknoll, N.Y.: Orbis Books, 1983).

CHAPTER 5

1. Most prominent is the work of Childs, *Introduction*, 325–38. See esp. the careful work of Ronald E. Clements, "Unity"; and idem, "Beyond Tradition-History: Deutero-Isaianic Development of First Isaiah's Themes," *Journal for the Study of the Old Testament* 31 (1985): 95–113. See also Brueggemann, "Unity and Dynamic in the Isaiah Tradition," *Journal for the Study of the Old Testament* 29 (1984): 89–107.

2. Martin Luther, "The Babylonian Captivity of the Church," in *Three Treatises* (Philadelphia: Fortress Press, 1960), 115–260.

3. On the general field of the metaphor of exile, see Ralph Klein, *Israel in Exile*. On a contemporary use of the metaphor as it has been filtered through the Book of Revelation, see William Stringfellow, *An Ethic for Christians and Other Aliens in a Strange Land* (Waco, Tex.: Word Books, 1973).

4. I regard the two recent letters of the American Roman Catholic bishops concerning nuclear arms and economics as an indirect appeal to a situation of exile. In ever such a gentle way, the bishops have asserted that the church in America now lives in a context whose values are fundamentally in tension with the claims of the church's faith.

5. See my discussion of this function of poetry in the prophets in *The Prophetic Imagination* (Philadelphia: Fortress Press, 1978).

6. On the power of Jesus' stories to break and dismantle the dominant reality, see John Dominic Crossan, *The Dark Interval*. Crossan's book reflects an important direction of scholarship, derived especially from the work of Amos Wilder and Paul Ricoeur.

7. Sallie McFague (*Metaphorical Theology*) has shown how the metaphor of "Kingdom of God" stands at the center of the biblical tradition and represents a threatening, inviting alternative of every kingdom "of this age."

8. On the capacity of King to use the old tradition in imaginative, poetic

ways for the sake of the present, see James H. Smylie, "On Jesus, Pharaohs, and the Chosen People," *Interpretation* 24 (1970): 74–91.

9. On the cruciality of a universe of discourse, see Herbert Marcuse, *One-Dimensional Man* (Boston: Beacon Press, 1964), chap. 4. The work of Stanley Hauerwas in *A Community of Character* (Notre Dame: Univ. of Notre Dame Press, 1981) and in many of his works indicates this cruciality.

10. Karl Barth has insisted that one must begin with what is *real* and then work from there to what is *possible*. When the movement is inverted, as it is in most liberal theology, imperial definitions of what is possible are at the outset determinative of what is real.

11. The appeal to the tradition made by 2 Isaiah, has been well documented by Bernhard Anderson: "Exodus Typology in Second Isaiah," in *Israel's Prophetic Heritage* (New York: Harper & Row, 1962), 177–95; idem, "Exodus and Covenant in Second Isaiah and Prophetic Tradition," *Magnalia Dei, The Mighty Acts of God,* ed. F. M. Cross, W. E. Lemke, and P. D. Miller, Jr. (Garden City, N.Y.: Doubleday & Co., 1976), 339–60.

12. On this text, see Brueggemann, "Will Our Faith Have Children?" *Word and World* 3 (1983): 272–83.

13. See Otto Eissfeldt, "The Promises of Grace of David in Isaiah 55:1–5," in *Israel's Prophetic Heritage,* 196–207. Richard J. Clifford, "Isaiah 55: Invitation to a Feast," in *The Word of the Lord Shall Go Forth,* 27–35, takes issue with Eissfeldt's thesis of democratization but shows in yet another way how the Davidic tradition serves as hope for the generation of exile.

14. For mapping of the form, see Claus Westermann, "The Way of the Promise Through the Old Testament," in *The Old Testament and Christian Faith,* ed. B. W. Anderson (New York: Harper & Row, 1963), 200–224. See Westermann's more detailed analysis in "Sprache und Struktur der Prophetie Deuterojesajas," *Forschung am alten Testament* (Munich: Kaiser Verlag, 1964), 117–24. See the more recent discussion of Edgar W. Conrad, "The 'Fear Not' Oracles in Second Isaiah," *Vetus Testamentum* 34 (1984): 129–52; idem, *Fear Not Warrior,* Brown Judaic Studies 75 (Chico, Calif.: Scholars Press, 1985).

15. Frank M. Cross, "The Council of Yahweh in Second Isaiah," *Journal of Near Eastern Studies* 12 (1953): 274–77.

16. On the importance of the divine council, see Patrick D. Miller, Jr., *Genesis 1—11* (Sheffield: JSOT Press, 1978), chap. 1.

CHAPTER 6

1. On the scholarly consensus concerning the historical setting of 2 Isaiah, see Ralph W. Klein, *Israel in Exile.*

2. On exiles as the bearer of Judaism's future, see Brueggemann, "A Second Reading of Jeremiah after the Dismantling," *Ex Auditu* 1 (1985):

156–68; and David N. Freedman, "The Biblical Idea of History," *Interpretation* 21 (1967): 32–49.

3. On the salvation oracles, see Westermann, "Sprache und Struktur," 117–20; and his derivative theological comments in, "The Way of the Promise through the Old Testament," in *The Old Testament and Christian Faith,* 200–224. See the recent critical comment of Edgar W. Conrad, "Second Isaiah and the Priestly Oracle of Salvation," *Zeitschrift für die alttestamentliche Wissenschaft* 93 (1981): 234–46.

4. See Westermann, "Sprache und Struktur," 124–44; and more generally his *Basic Forms of Prophetic Speech* (Philadelphia: Westminster Press, 1967).

5. On this intergenerational issue, see Michael Fishbane, *Text and Texture* (New York: Schocken Books, 1979), 78–83; and Brueggemann, "The Family as World-Maker," *Journal for Preachers* 7 (Easter 1985): 8–15.

6. On the reality and tension of two theological traditions, see Brueggemann, "Trajectories in Old Testament Literature and the Sociology of Ancient Israel," *Journal of Biblical Literature* 98 (1979): 161–85.

7. Bernhard W. Anderson, "Exodus Typology in Second Isaiah"; idem, "Exodus and Covenant in Second Isaiah and Prophetic Tradition," has fully explored the use of the tradition by 2 Isaiah. On the other hand, Brevard S. Childs, *Introduction,* 325–38; and Ronald Clements, "Unity," have placed a very different reading on the notion of "newness" in this poetry.

8. On this text and its future, see Brueggemann, "'Impossibility' and Epistemology," 615–34.

9. John van Seters, *Abraham in History and Tradition* (New Haven, Conn.: Yale Univ. Press, 1975), has made the judgment that these narratives themselves do not constitute evidence for an old memory. While his hypothesis has a certain rationality, there is an inherent improbability in it.

10. On the power of the Sarah tradition as a source of hope, see Brueggemann, "Will Our Faith Have Children?"

11. On the model expressed in this psalm, see Norman Whybray, *The Second Isaiah* (Sheffield: JSOT Press, 1983), 30–34.

12. See the discussion of Peter Berger and Thomas Luckmann, *The Social Construction of Reality,* 156–63.

13. On v. 15, see the shrewd statement by Emil Fackenheim, "New Hearts and the Old Covenant: On Some Possibilities of a Fraternal Jewish Christian Reading of the Jewish Bible Today."

14. On the compassion of God, see Monica Hellweg, *Jesus, The Compassion of God* (Wilmington, Del.: Michael Glazier, 1983).

15. On the problem of continuity and discontinuity, see Peter R. Ackroyd, "Continuity and Discontinuity: Rehabilitation and Authentication," in *Tradition and Theology in the Old Testament,* ed. D. A. Knight (Philadelphia: Fortress Press, 1977), 215–34.

16. Against the scholarly consensus, see Childs, *Introduction,* 216–25; and

Ronald Clements, "Unity." See my comments in "Unity and Dynamic in Isaiah," 89–107.

17. Cf. Morris Silver, *Prophets and Markets,* 225, 227.

18. On such a notion informed by philosophical idealism, see Paul Tillich, *The Eternal Now* (New York: Charles Scribner's Sons, 1963), in which Tillich tries to escape the reality of historical process.

19. On the various ways in which Old and New Testaments relate through historical memory, see A. S. Gunneweg, *Understanding the Old Testament* (Philadelphia: Westminster Press, 1978).

20. On the promise, see Claus Westermann, *The Promises to the Fathers* (Philadelphia: Fortress Press, 1980); and David J. A. Clines, *The Theme of the Pentateuch* (Sheffield: JSOT Press, 1978), esp. 32–43.

21. On the social radicalness of the gospel of Luke, see Juan Luis Segundo, *The Historical Jesus of the Synoptics* (Maryknoll, N.Y.: Orbis Books, 1985).

22. On the history of the narrative process which has lost the power of narrative and transposed narrative into a mode of social control, see Hans Frei, *The Eclipse of Biblical Narrative* (New Haven: Yale University Press, 1974).

23. On the radical and passionate claims of the core tradition, see Walter Harrelson, "Life, Faith, and the Emergence of Tradition," in *Tradition and Theology in the Old Testament,* 11–30.

24. Alice Walker, *In Search of Our Mothers' Gardens* (New York: Harcourt Brace Jovanovich, 1983), 5.

CONCLUSION

1. On such a contextualization, see Hauerwas, *Community;* and Stringfellow, *Ethic for Christians.*

2. On the pertinence of a theology of the cross to our social situation, see Douglas Hall, *Lighten Our Darkness* (Philadelphia: Westminster Press, 1976).

PUBLISHER'S NOTE

British editions of books cited in the notes have been published as follows:

Peter Ackroyd, *Exile and Restoration*, SCM Press
B. W. Anderson, *The Old Testament and Christian Faith*, SCM Press
Peter Berger, *The Heretical Imperative*, Collins
Brevard S. Childs, *Introduction to the Old Testament as Scripture*, SCM Press
Norman K. Gottwald, *The Tribes of Yahweh*, SCM Press
A. H. J. Gunneweg, *Understanding the Old Testament*, SCM Press
Gustavo Gutiérrez, *The Power of the Poor in History*, SCM Press
Kazo Kitamori, *Theology of the Pain of God*, SCM Press
Sallie McFague, *Metaphorical Theology*, SCM Press
Alasdair MacIntyre, *After Virtue*, Duckworth
Herbert Marcuse, *One Dimensional Man*, Routledge
Gerhard von Rad, *Old Testament Theology*, SCM Press
Eduard Schweizer, *The Good News according to Luke*, SPCK
Paul Tillich, *The Eternal Now*, SCM Press
Paul Tournier, *The Strong and the Weak*, SCM Press